Classic Carving Projects Made Easy

Bottle Stoppers

by Greg Young

Fox Chapel Publishing Co. Inc.
1970 Broad Street • East Petersburg, PA 17520 • www.foxchapelpublishing.com

Acknowledgments

This book, this labor of love, would have never come to fruition were it not for the constant support of my family. Their love has surrounded me throughout this endeavor; so I give thanks from the bottom of my heart to my wife, Grace; my son, Justin; my daughter, Gabrielle; and my wonderful extended family. Thanks!

It is with a great deal of humility and gratitude that I say thanks to Ayleen Stellhorn, who has been a gentle guide along the way, to Alan Giagnocavo and to the entire team at Fox Chapel Publishing for this great opportunity that has been offered to me. You folks are indeed a class act, and I am honored to become one of your team. Thanks!

I got my start teaching woodcarving at the Woodcraft store in West Allis, Wisconsin, and all the step-by-step photos for the book were photographed there. Thanks so much to Chris, Deana, Steve and the rest of the gang at Woodcraft for your encouragement, support and accommodation!

The marvelous step-by-step photos found in this book were a true labor of love shot by a great friend and carving student of mine, Mark Zielinski. Thank you so much!

Finally, to the wonderful, gentle man who was the brother that I never had—the late Dr. Kim Burch—and his family. Kim, this one's for you!

Publisher	Alan Giagnocavo
Book Editor	Ayleen Stellhorn
Interior Photography	Harry Troutman
Step-by-Step Photography	Mark Zielinski
Cover Design	David Marty
Layout and Design	Linda L. Eberly

ISBN 1-56523-144-9
Library of Congress Preassigned Card Number: 2002114665

To order your copy of this book,
please send check or money order
for the cover price plus $3.50 shipping to:
Fox Chapel Publishing Company, Inc.
Book Orders
1970 Broad St.
East Petersburg, PA 17520

Or visit us on the web at *www.foxchapelpublishing.com*

Printed in China
10 9 8 7 6 5 4 3 2 1

Table of Contents

Santa
page 64

Heart
page 24

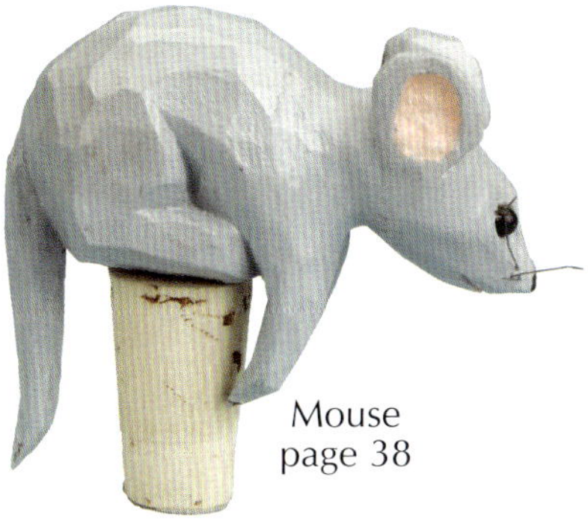

Mouse
page 38

Introduction

Several years ago, when I was relatively fresh out of seminary, my wife, Grace, and I accepted a six-month interim call to a church in International Falls, Minnesota. While there, you might say that I met "joy." Joy personified came in the diminutive form of a very elderly lady, whose name now, I'm embarrassed to say, I don't recall. But she would like the name Joy, because it fit her. When I first met her after conducting my first Sunday worship service at the church, she was overjoyed that I had quoted some of her favorite literary giants. This lady—and truly she was indeed a lady—was well read and dressed quite formally when coming to church, replete with hat and gloves to match. You might have thought her stuffy with her command of the King's English and formal attire, but she was not. I soon discovered that this outer appearance was only a guise.

I'll never forget early one Sunday morning, well before the scheduled church service was to begin, the choir was practicing in the sanctuary; and this dear lady about whom I now write, was sitting there, having been dropped off early at church by her driver. She could hear well, but her eyesight was very poor. The choir was practicing some peppy, joyful piece of music. To my amazement, this refined, dignified, elderly lady dressed in her long white gloves and hat was kicking up her legs and moving her arms in time to the music as if she were one of the Rockettes. She was oblivious to her surroundings, oblivious to that internal censor that says, "What will people think?"

I do know what I thought and felt watching her, but one word captures it well: Joy. Although this delightful lady didn't know it, she had given me a very precious gift that day, a gift of joy.

But that was not the entire lesson on joy as it turns out. The other portion of that lesson came for me just before Grace and I left at the end of my six-month ministry there to accept a call at a church in northern Michigan. A few days before leaving, I stopped up to see this fine lady and say goodbye. It was October, and the first things I noticed upon entering her apartment were all the Christmas decorations. Her apartment was filled with Christmas trees, colored lights, garlands, ornaments, nativity sets, angels and lots of Santas.

During the course of our conversation, I asked her about all the Christmas decorations. I'll never forget her response. She said, "I keep them up all year long to remind everyone who comes to visit me that the spirit of Christmas should be celebrated every day of the year, that we should be joyful, happy and hopeful."

And this is the theme that I would like to run throughout this book, one of joy. People have asked me from time to time why I like to carve. Aside from the most common response of creative expression, perhaps the most compelling reason is the joy that woodcarving brings to me: I find joy in completing a woodcarving that pleases me; I find joy in seeing the eyes of people light up with joy when visiting my booth at an art show; I find joy in teaching others how to carve something that they are proud of (I don't know who is prouder in such instances, my students or me); and finally, I find joy in being able to share what I do and create with others.

Bottle stoppers are associated with joyous and festive occasions—birthdays, Christmas, Easter, Halloween, St. Patrick's Day, Valentine's Day, July Fourth, the coming of spring, the change of seasons and so on. If carving these stopper projects brings a smile to your face and to the faces of those close to you, then the creation of this book will have been well worth the effort for me.

Enjoy,
Greg Young

Editor's Note: You can reach Greg directly by mail at W160 N9693 Colonial Drive, Germantown, WI 53022, or by e-mail: *winslowlake@wi.rr.com*. His website address is *www.gregyoungcarvings.com.*

Bottle Stopper Basics

I have included a broad range of carving projects in this book. Many of these projects are fun and easy to do; some are a bit more challenging. Beginning carvers should start with the simpler projects such as the Bow Tie Snowman on page 18, the Heart Stopper on page 24 and the Chilly Penguin on page 42. As you become more comfortable with your carving skills, try the Wind-Swept Santa on page 66 or Uncle Sam on page 58.

Some of the stopper projects call for a few special materials to complete the project. All of these materials are readily available and are noted on the pattern for that particular project.

Wood Choice

I used basswood for the bottle stoppers. Basswood is a preferred carving wood because it has a tight uniform grain and is relatively soft, even though it is considered a hardwood. Because of the tight, fine grain, basswood accepts fine carving detail well.

Most of the basswood available to purchase is kiln-dried. The best place to purchase basswood carving blocks is through a woodcarving or woodworking store. If there isn't a store near you, most of the woodcarving supply stores sell their products by mail order. You can locate a mail-order company by doing a search on the Internet or by checking out the advertisements in your favorite carving magazine. Members of your local woodcarving club are also great sources of information on finding and buying wood.

Bottle stoppers also look great with a natural finish. Try a wood with a more pronounced grain, such as butternut. Butternut is related to walnut. It has a rich, beautiful grain. As a carving wood, it is a little harder to carve than basswood; but it is still relatively easy to carve and it accepts fine carving detail well.

Another wood that a beginning woodcarver might want to consider is sugar pine. This wood possesses similar characteristics to basswood. Sugar pine and many other varieties of wood can be purchased through the same sources as basswood.

I encourage all beginning woodcarvers to learn more about various kinds of wood and how easy or difficult these various species are to carve. R. Bruce Hoadley has written two books, *Understanding Wood* and *Identifying Wood*, which are very helpful resources. Peter Bishop's book, *100 Woods: A Guide to the Popular Timbers of the World*, is also a good resource for more information on wood.

A Word About Tools

There are a number of good woodcarving tools on the market. If you are a beginning woodcarver,

Pictured here are the key stages in the carving of the snowman stopper project. Basswood is a relatively easy wood to carve and holds details well.

purchase a few good quality tools to begin carving. Your initial tool list should include:

- a bench knife
- a ¼" v-tool (for texturing and creating stop cuts)
- a medium width, medium sweep gouge (ie: 10 mm #7 palm gouge or a ⅝" #3 palm gouge)

There are a number of sources available for finding and purchasing quality woodcarving tools. If you live in an area that has a good woodworking store, do some comparison shopping there with the help of a salesperson. There are also mail-order woodcarving supply stores that offer woodcarving tools for sale through their catalogs and website addresses. Finally, find out if a woodcarving club meets in your area. The members are often invaluable resources for inside information on tools.

Any tool you purchase should be made from good quality steel and have a reputation for holding a razor sharp cutting edge over extended use. Also select a tool that feels comfortable to hold in your hand.

As a beginning carver, you will want to purchase a good bench knife first. There are many sizes and shapes of woodcarving knives on the market. I recommend that your first knife has a pointed tip for doing detail work and a straight cutting edge.

A Note About Sharpening

I believe that it is important for beginning woodcarvers to start out with tools that have been pre-sharpened. These tools will provide the beginner with a "benchmark" of how a truly sharp tool easily cuts through wood. Sharp tools are a joy to use; dull tools will often lead to frustration and discouragement for the beginning carver. Dull tools are also more dangerous to use because the carver must apply more force to the tool to execute the cut, which leads to a greater danger of losing control of the tool, which can lead to injury.

As a general rule of thumb, I sharpen my tools every 30 to 40 minutes on a leather strop coated with chromium oxide. I only use a sharpening stone if I have damaged the cutting edge of the tool.

You will want to learn how to sharpen your carving tools properly. Learning how to sharpen your tools is perhaps just as important as selecting the quality tools themselves. There are several excellent books and videotapes that will instruct you on how to

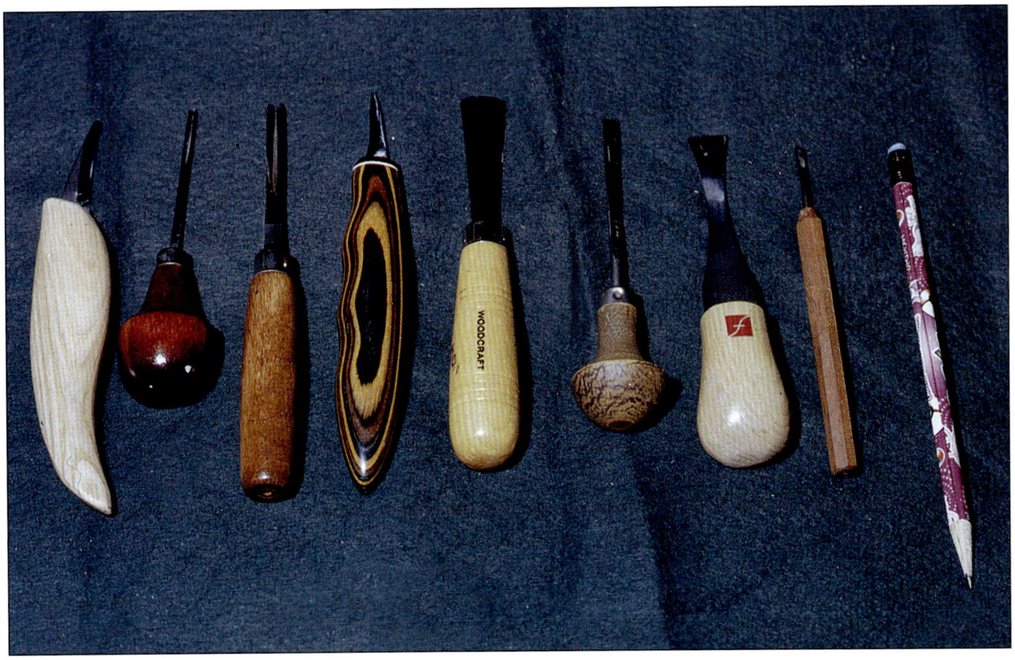

A good quality carving knife with a sharp tip and a straight cutting edge (fourth from left) is the most important tool for carving bottle stoppers. Other tools may be helpful, but are not necessary.

sharpen and maintain a keen cutting edge on all your carving tools. *How to Sharpen Tools* by Rick Butz and *Sharpening Basics* by Patrick Spielman are very good resources. As you become more experienced in woodcarving and acquire more tools, consider purchasing a copy of *The Complete Guide to Sharpening* by Leonard Lee. This book is technical in nature and a great resource for those who want to explore a variety of sharpening options.

Pattern Notes

I keep master files of my various carving patterns. When I want to use a pattern, I trace it on a piece of tracing paper. To transfer that pattern to a block of wood, I place a piece of carbon paper (transfer paper also works well) under the pattern and use masking tape to secure the corners. I then carefully trace over the pattern lines with a pen or pencil. If I plan to use a pattern repeatedly, I trace the pattern to clear acetate because it is more durable than tracing paper.

As you lay out the patterns, be sure that the wood grain travels the length of the pattern. Wood grain refers to the bundled fibers that run parallel to each other up and down the length of the tree. In the beginner woodcarving classes that I teach, I will often hold up a straw broom to illustrate the flow of wood grain through a block of wood and what it means to carve with and against the grain. To ensure strength, make sure that any thin pattern pieces run the length of the wood grain and not across the grain.

After the pattern has been laid out, be sure to mark the bottom center of the project and drill a ⅜" hole to accommodate the dowel and the cork stopper.

Basic Carving Cuts

As all of the carving students that I have taught would testify, I want to stress the importance of making clean, accurate stop cuts. It is so easy to want to pick at a piece of wood that doesn't come out cleanly from a stop cut; but excess picking often leads to stop cut areas that have a multitude of frayed wood fibers, also knows as "fuzzies." These fuzzies will blur the carved area that you are trying to define.

In addition to learning to make good stop cuts, it is important to learn what's commonly referred to as slicing cuts. These cuts require good safety techniques. A general rule of thumb is to carve away from your body whenever you can. Another important rule is to use only wrist action of the hand holding the carving tool to execute the cut. This gives you far better control over the carving tool and is much safer.

It is also important to use the thumb on the hand holding the piece of wood being carved as a pivot and brace on the spine of the carving blade. This may seem awkward at first, but once you learn to use the thumb to help control the carving blade, you can execute much more controlled and precise cuts.

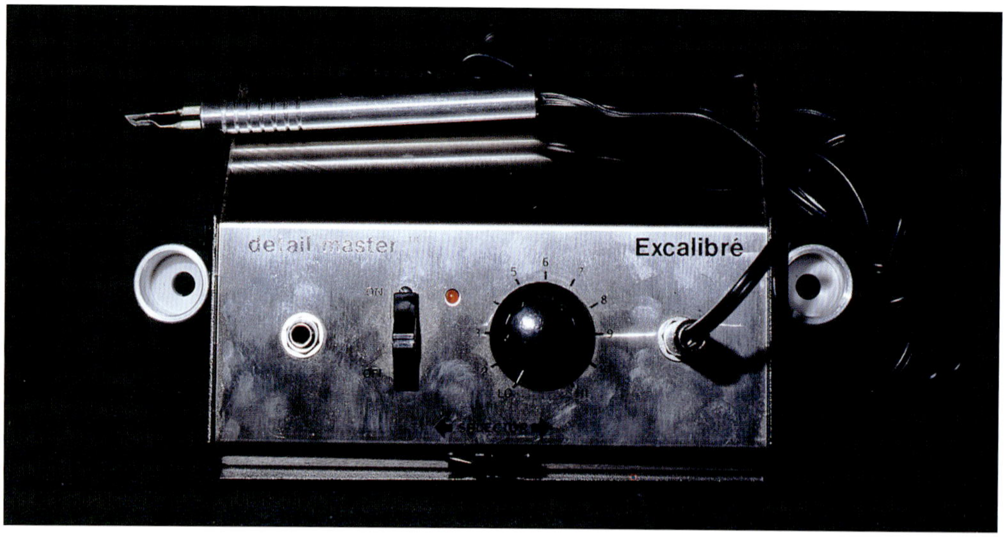

A woodburning pen provides an alternate way to add many details, such as facial features, fur texture, hair and more.

All of the painted projects in this book are painted with acrylic paints. Generic colors are listed for each project. Any similar color from any of the brands of acrylic paint on the market will work well. Try attaching the dowel to the piece before you begin painting. It will serve as a handy way to hold the carving while it's being painted.

Dry-brushing is a special painting technique that will give additional interest to your painting. To dry-brush, dip a fairly stiff-bristled paint brush in a small pool of paint; then wipe most of the paint off on a clean, dry paper towel. Lightly flutter the brush back and forth over the areas that you want dry-brushed. Dry-brushing adds depth to the painting by further defining the carving tool marks and toning down the intense color of the acrylic paints. After the paint has dried, seal the project with an acrylic sealer.

Antiquing is an optional step and will give your project a nice old-fashioned finish. To antique a project, spray the dried, sealed piece with a golden oak stain. After spraying the piece, immediately follow up by wiping off the stain with a lint-free cloth or soft paper towel. Allow the piece to dry thoroughly.

As you will notice, many of the finished examples in this book show the deep tool cuts used to carve the piece. I especially like this effect—it adds a dimension and depth to the painted project—and I purposefully do very little or no sanding to keep those marks apparent. If you would like to duplicate this effect, you will need to work with very sharp tools that will give you smooth cuts.

Sanding and Finishing

Several of the stopper projects in this book shouldn't need to be sanded prior to finishing, providing that your tools are very sharp and that you use good cutting techniques. Some of the projects, however, call for a smoother surface and can be sanded to achieve that effect. Note: Avoid using a carving tool on an area that you have just sanded because the sanding abrasive left on the wood surface will damage your tools.

If you need to sand, I recommend a 320-grit sandpaper, as it leaves a fairly smooth surface. After sanding, seal the project with an acrylic sealer, such as Deft, before you paint.

Assemble the acrylic paints and brushes needed before you begin to paint a project.

Attaching a Cork

In selecting cork for these bottle stopper projects, I found it much easier to purchase corks that have already been cut. Many woodcarving stores and catalogs offer pre-drilled corks for bottle stoppers. The

FITTING THE CORK

The bottle stoppers in this book are carved from basswood, then attached to a cork stopper. Cork stoppers can be bought pre-cut and pre-drilled from many carving supply stores.

Insert a 3/8" hardwood dowel into the hole in the bottom of the stopper. (The hole is drilled prior to any carving work.) This will help you to hold the piece while you paint, and later, it will hold the cork tightly in place.

Measure the cork against the dowel...

...and cut off any unneeded length.

Use several drops of super glue on the cork and insert the dowel into the cork.

The cork fits tightly against the stopper.

All of the stoppers in this book were painted with acrylic paint and sealed with a matte finish spray.

hole size of the pre-drilled corks is 3/8" and accommodates the 3/8" dowels called for in the bill of materials for each project.

Before attaching the cork, mark the portion of the dowel that extends beyond the bottom of the stopper and cut it off so that the dowel is flush with the stopper bottom. Glue the stopper and dowel in place with wood glue or a good quality super-glue adhesive found at most woodworking stores.

Other Uses

Several of the stopper projects in this book will also make great holiday ornaments. To turn a bottle stopper into an ornament, simply skip the initial step of drilling the 3/8" dowel hole in the bottom of the project. Find and mark the balance point on the top of the completed carving; then screw a small brass eyelet into the balance point.

Stoppers can also be used creatively as chain pulls on ceiling fans and decorative finials on lamp shades. There is no end to the creative uses for these bottle stopper patterns.

Carving and Painting a Snowman Stopper

Carving a bottle stopper has as much to do with using a pencil as it does with using a knife. You'll note in the following demonstration, and throughout the projects that follow, that I use my pencil at just about every stage of the process. Don't be afraid to sketch out your cuts on the wood before you cut them with a knife. This trick will help you to visualize the cut. Also, be sure that you use a pencil and not a marker or a pen. Lead marks from a pencil can be carved or sanded away; ink from a marker or pen may sink into the wood and permanently color your carving.

Follow this demonstration step-by-step, referring often to the original pattern printed in this book. This demonstration covers all of the basic information you will need to carve the projects featured in the pattern section. Be willing to carve the same bottle stopper several times if you feel that your skills will benefit from the repetition. Also, be sure to keep your first bottle stopper carving. You'll want to look back on it at some point in the future to see just how much your carvings have improved.

TOOLS

Pencil
Bench knife
1/4" v-tool
1/8" v-tool
5/8" #3 palm gouge
Drill with 3/8" bit

MATERIALS

5" x 1 7/8" x 1 1/2" block of basswood
3/8"-diameter hardwood dowel, 3" long
1/8"-diameter hardwood dowel, 3/4" long
Cork stopper

PAINTS

White
Orange
Black cherry
Metallic gold
Hunter green
Black

PATTERN

CARVING

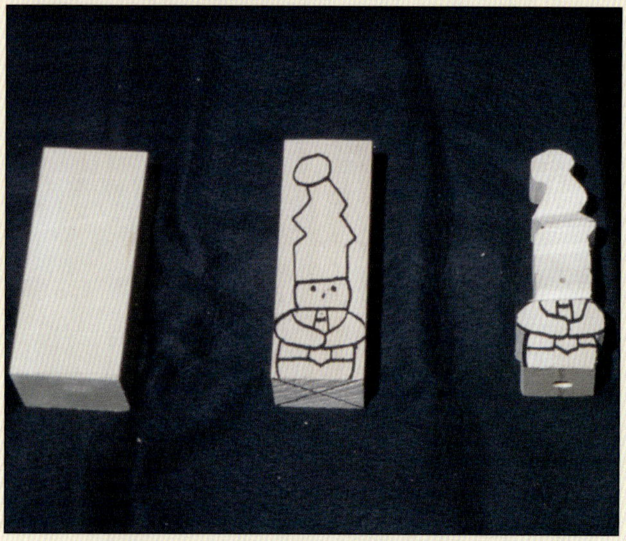

1 The wood used for this project is basswood. You will need a block that is 5″ long, 1 7/8″ wide and 1 1/2″ deep. Be sure the wood grain runs the length of the project. Transfer the pattern to the wood using carbon paper. Use a band saw, scroll saw or coping saw to cut the outline of the pattern. This is your cutout, or blank.

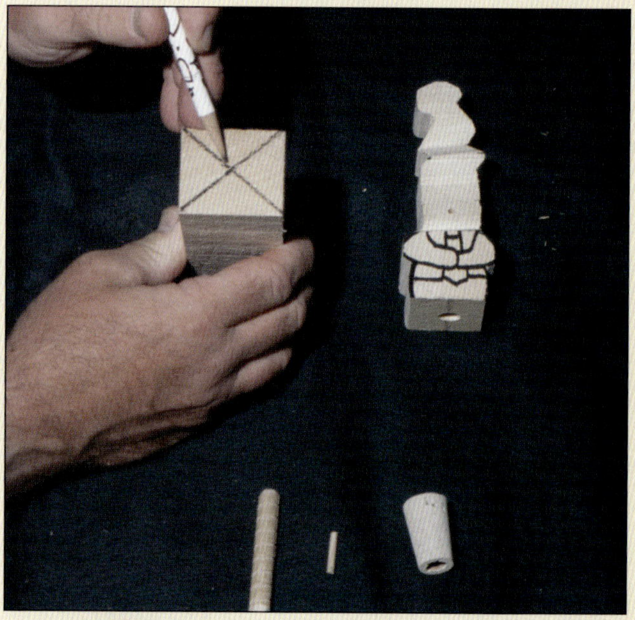

2 Draw an "x" from corner to corner on the bottom of the cutout. The center of the "x" marks the center of the base. Use a 3/8″ drill bit to drill a hole in the bottom to accommodate a 3/8″ hardwood dowel.

3 You will need the tools pictured here to complete this snowman bottle stopper: (left to right) a detail knife, a 1/8″ v-tool, a bench knife, a 1/4″ v-tool and a 5/8″ #3 palm gouge.

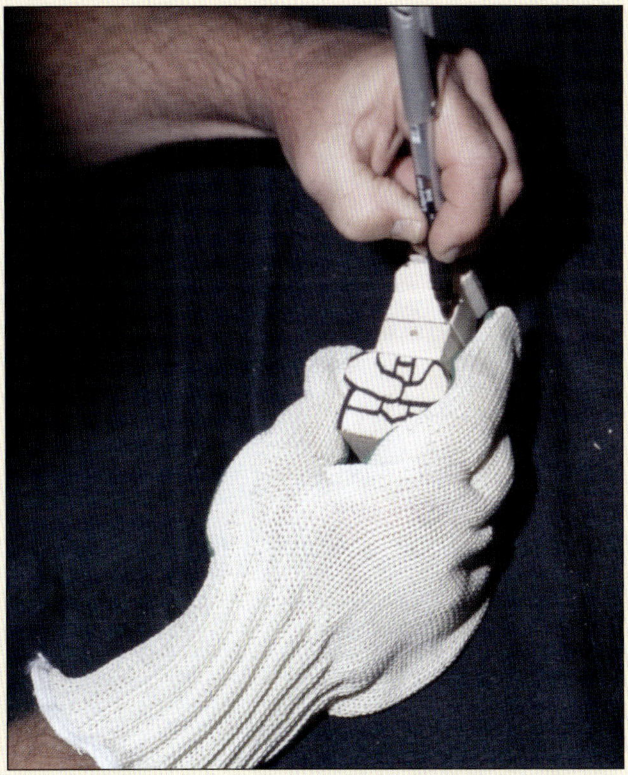

4 Using a pencil, draw the hat lines around the bottom of the hat and around the bottom of the ball on top of the hat.

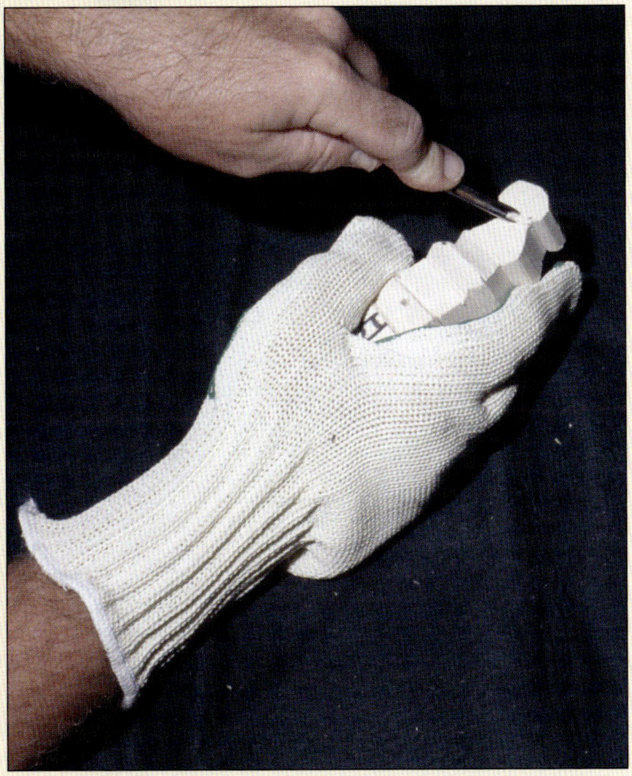

5 Using the 1/4″ v-tool, carve a stop cut separating the ball on the top of the hat from the hat itself. Follow the line you made in Step 3.

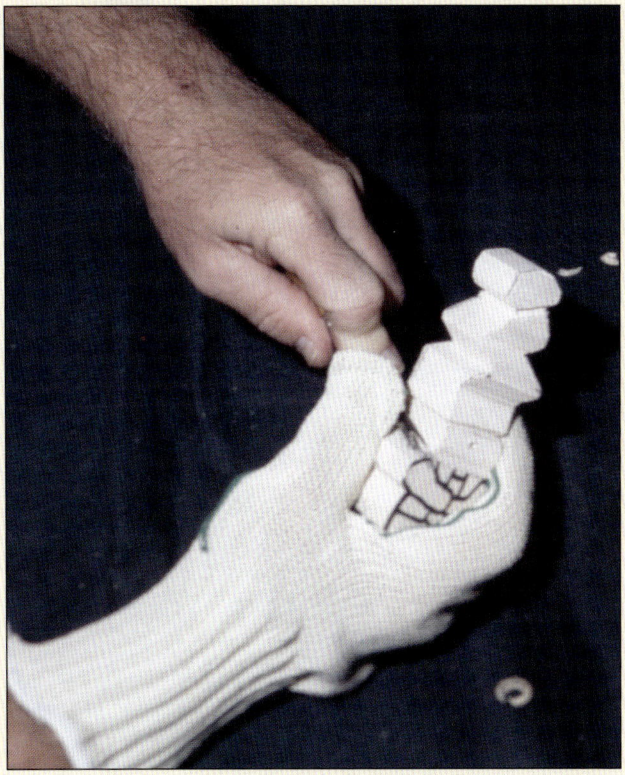

6 Using the same 1/4″ v-tool, carve a stop cut along the neck. Again, follow the line you made in Step 3.

7 With a bench knife, carve off the corners of the snowman. Be sure to carefully remove the corners of the hat as well.

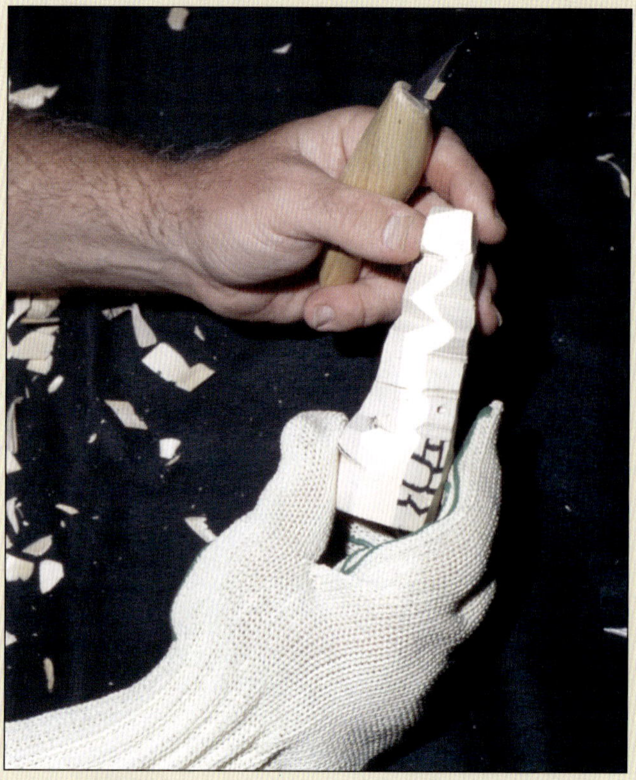

8 When Step 7 is complete, the snowman will look like this.

9 Use a pencil to reestablish the hat lines. Also draw in the top and bottom lines defining the snowman's arms.

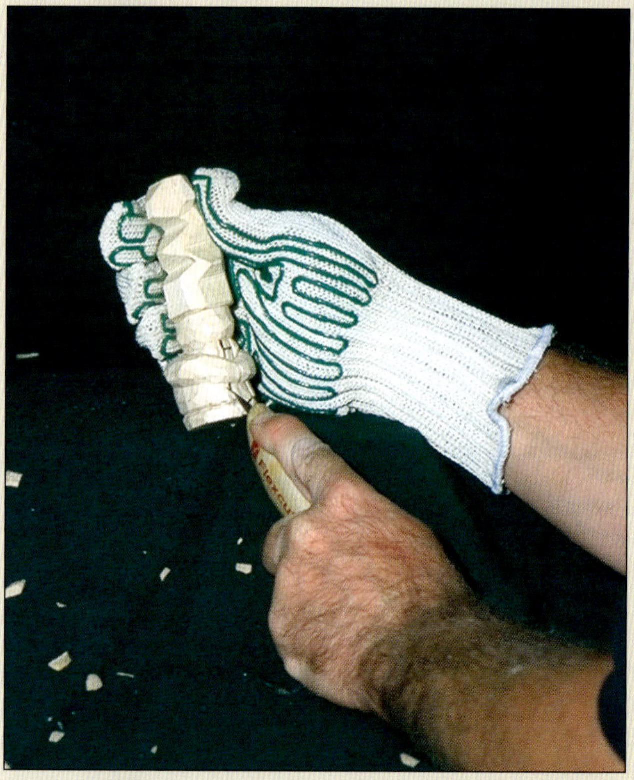

10 Use the 1/4″ v-tool to outline the tops and bottoms of the snowman's arms; then deepen those stop cuts with the bench knife.

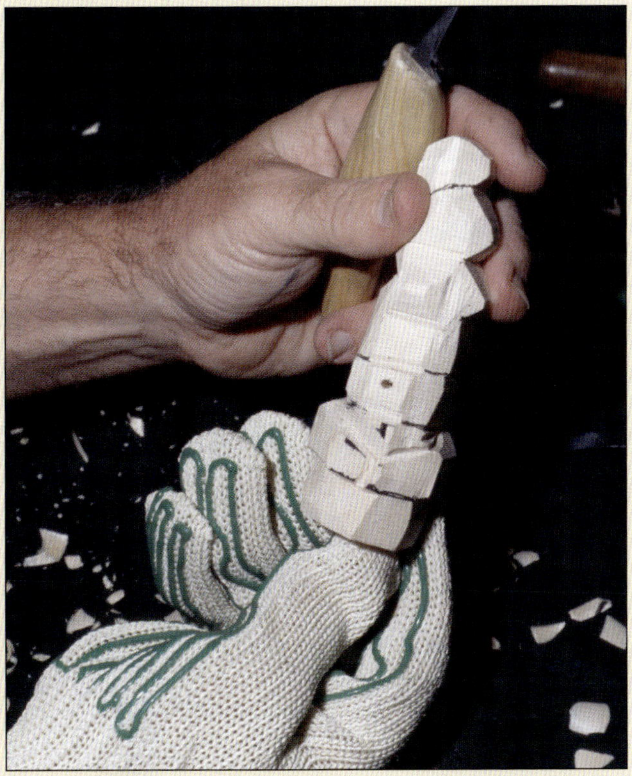

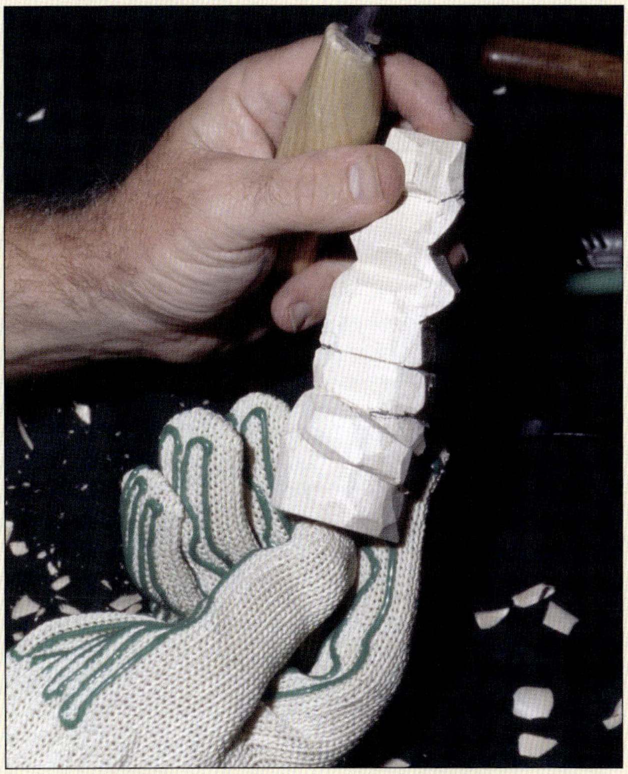

11 Use the bench knife to remove wood from above and below the arms to define the arms.

12 After completing Steps 10 and 11, the snowman should look like this.

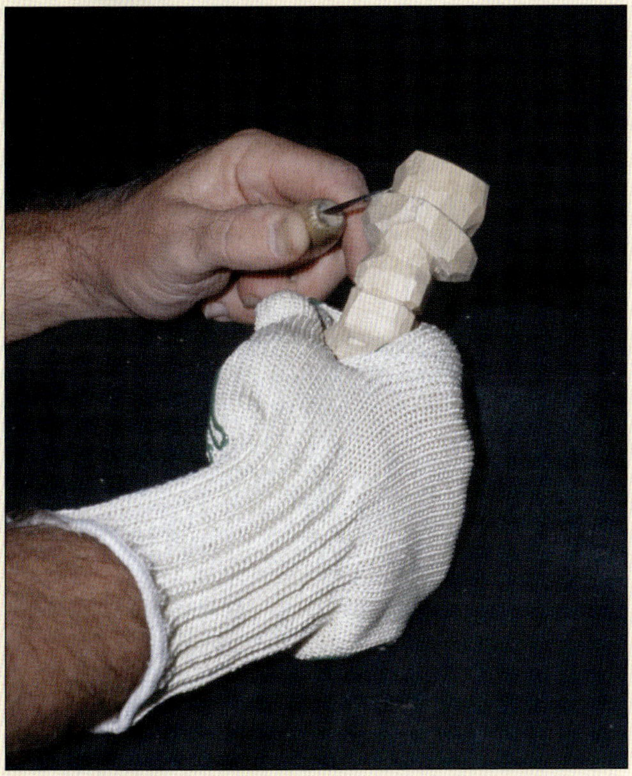

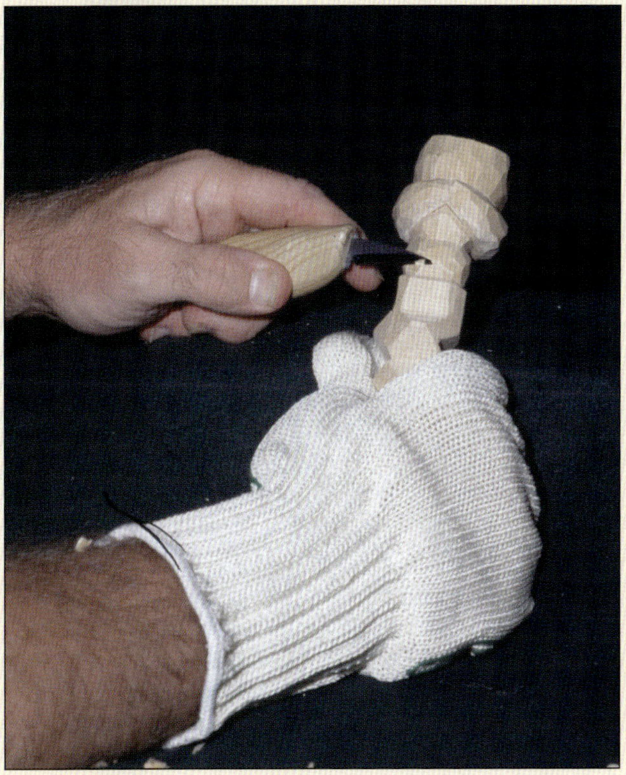

13 Turning the snowman as necessary, continue rounding and shaping the arms with the bench knife or the 5/8″ #3 palm gouge.

14 Holding the snowman upside down, round and shape the body up to the bottom of the hat using the bench knife or the 5/8″ #3 palm gouge. The stop cut you established in Step 5 will prevent you from cutting into the wood of the hat.

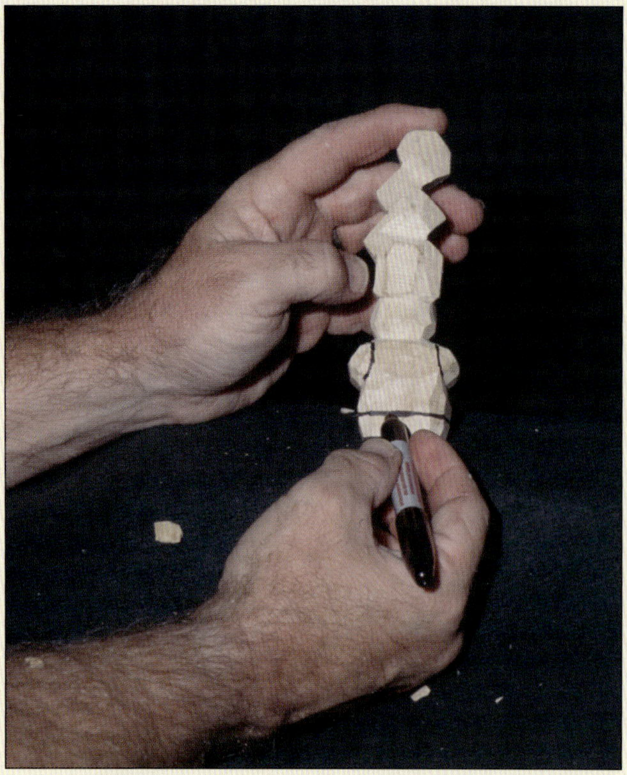

15 After shaping the snowman's body, use a pencil to draw in the snowman's vest. Use the pattern as a reference.

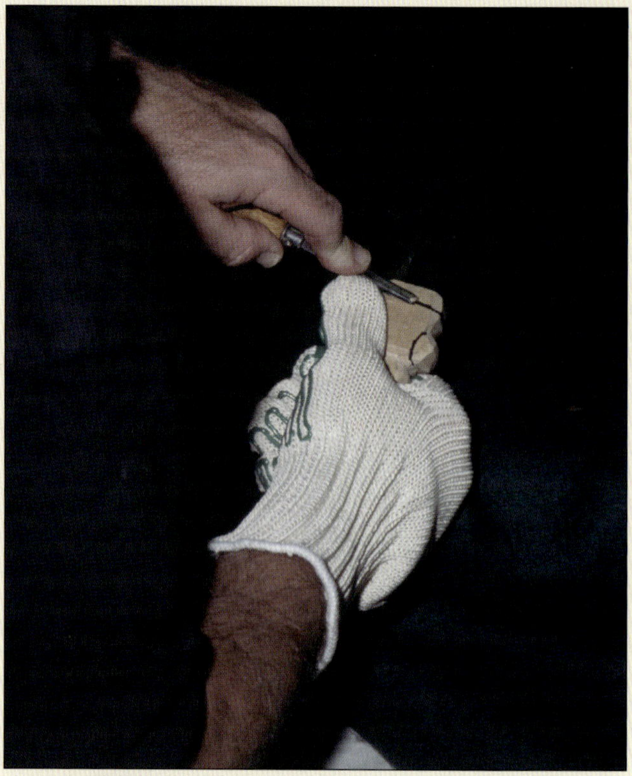

16 Cut the lines of the vest using the 1/4″ v-tool. This step will establish stop cuts along the edges of the vest where the vest meets the snowman's body.

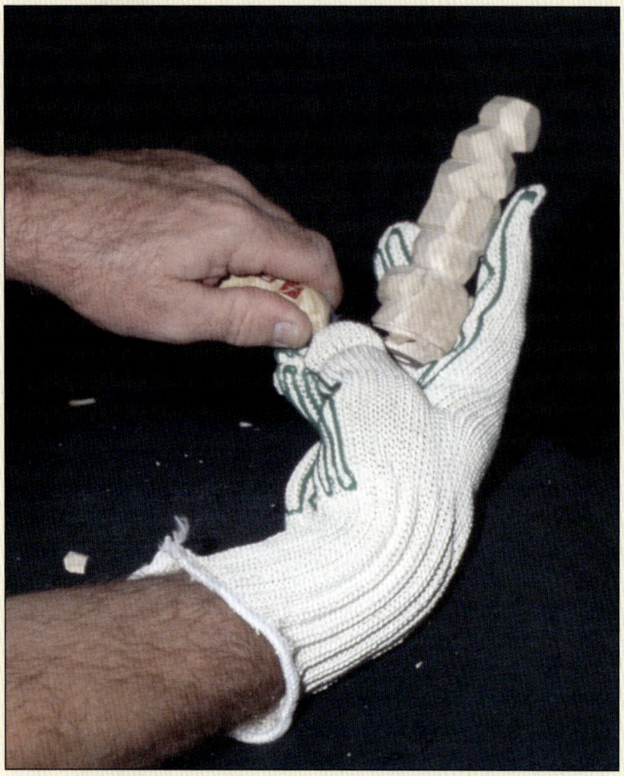

17 Use the bench knife or the 5/8″ #3 palm gouge to remove wood below the vest. These cuts will define the bottom of the vest.

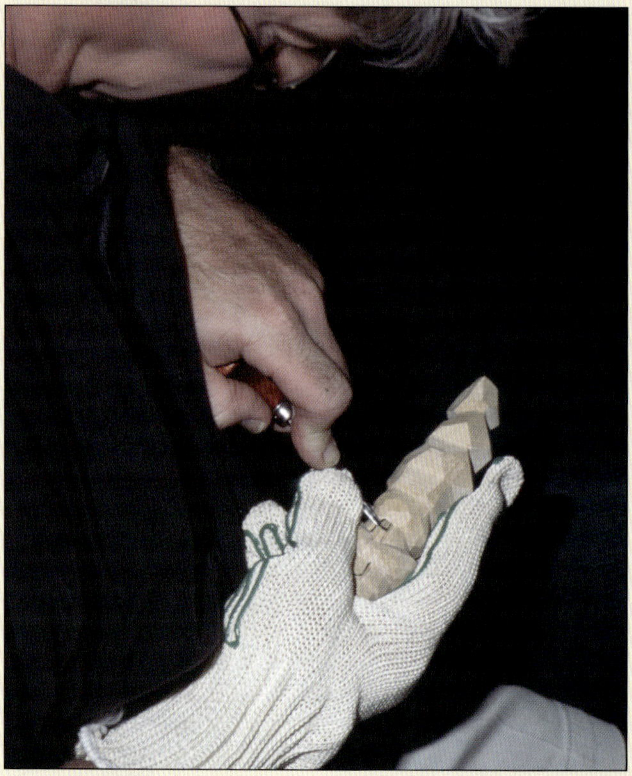

18 With the 1/8″ v-tool, carve along the lines of the snowman's tie. This will create stop cuts along these lines.

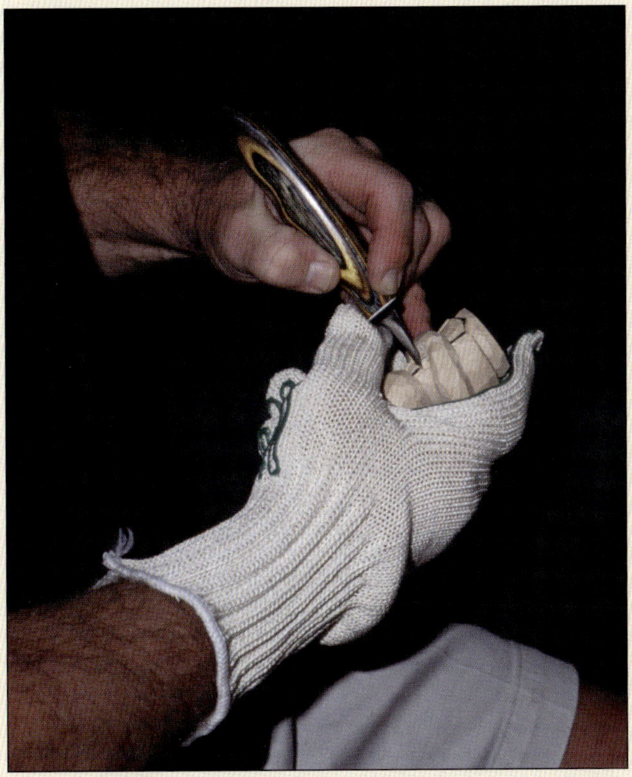

19 Deepen the stop cuts along the tie using the tip of the bench knife.

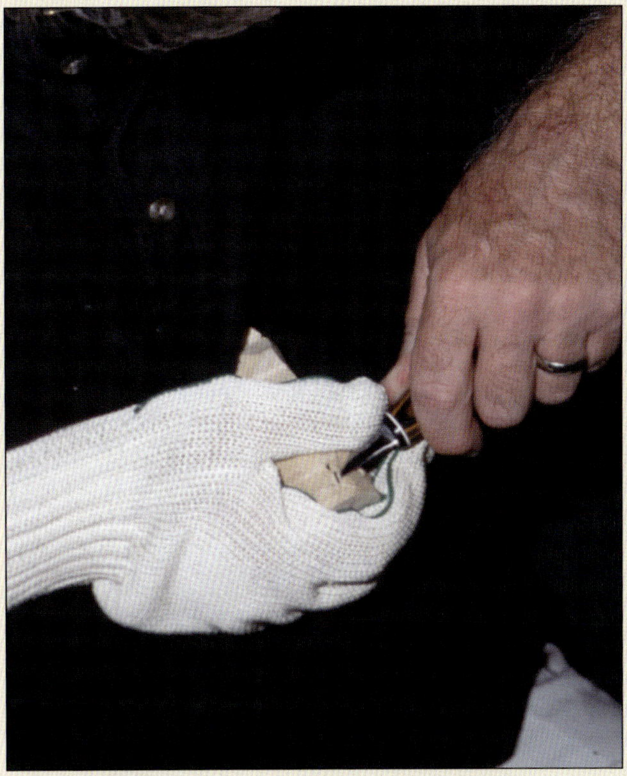

20 Holding the bench knife at a shallow angle, carve away a small amount of wood from the outside edges of the tie. These cuts will distinguish the tie from the vest.

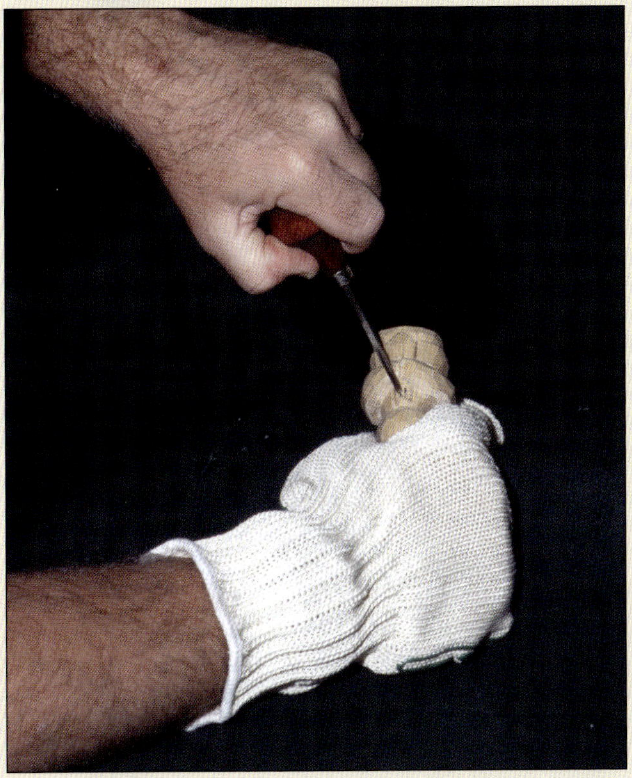

21 Carve and define the knot in the tie. Next carve several creases in the tie just below the knot.

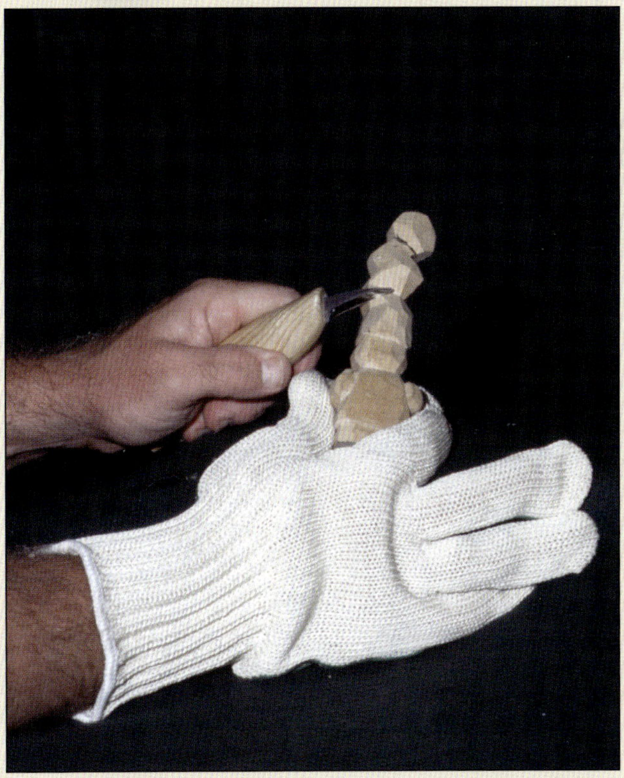

22 Using the bench knife, shape the hat up to the ball on the top of the hat. Remove small chips of wood until the hat is rounded.

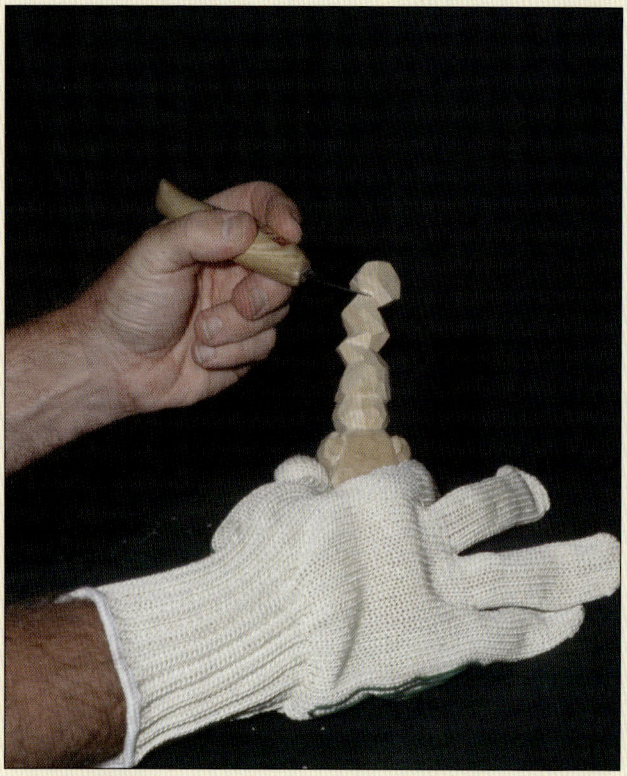

23 Still using the bench knife, round the ball of the hat.

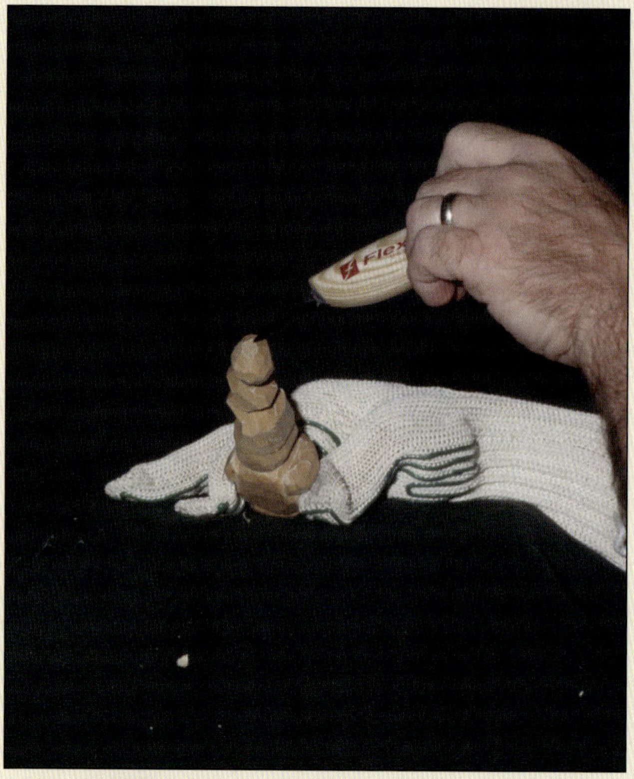

24 A view from the top of the snowman gives you a look at the final shape of the hat.

25 Use a pencil to mark the location of the nose.

26 Place a 1/8″ drill bit in a pin vise and carefully drill the hole for the nose.

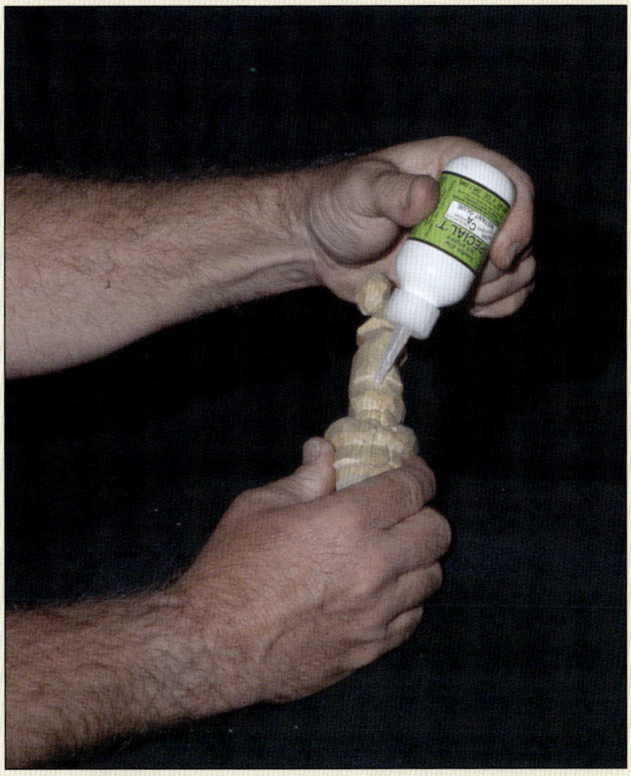

27 Place a drop of super glue in the nose hole.

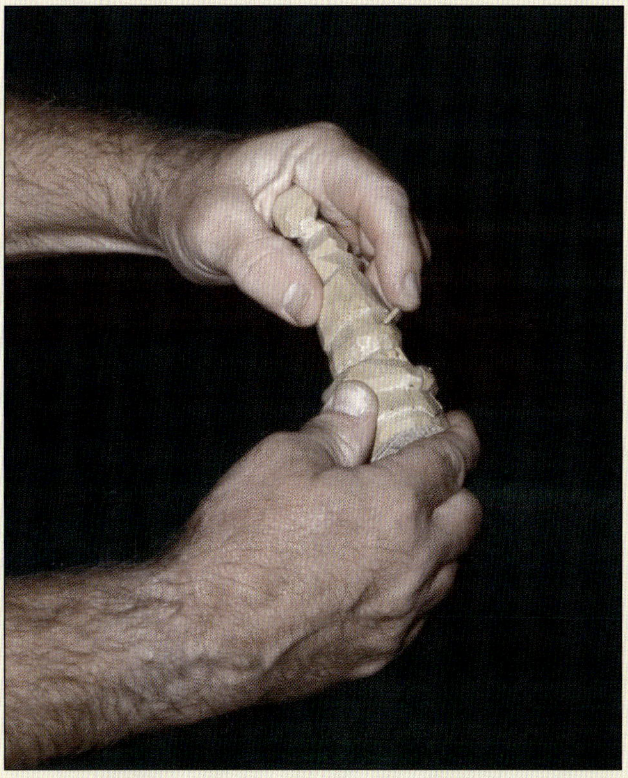

28 Insert the 3/4″ piece of 1/8″ dowel into the hole. After the glue dries, taper the tip of the nose using the bench knife.

Step-By-Step

PAINTING

1 Paint the snowman's head, arms and bottom white.

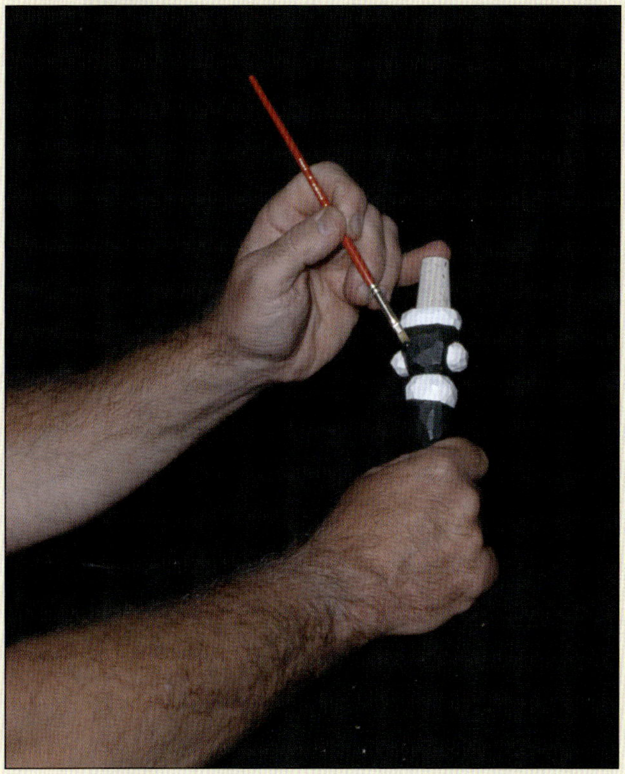

2 Paint the hat and vest hunter green.

3 Paint the snowman's nose with orange acrylic.

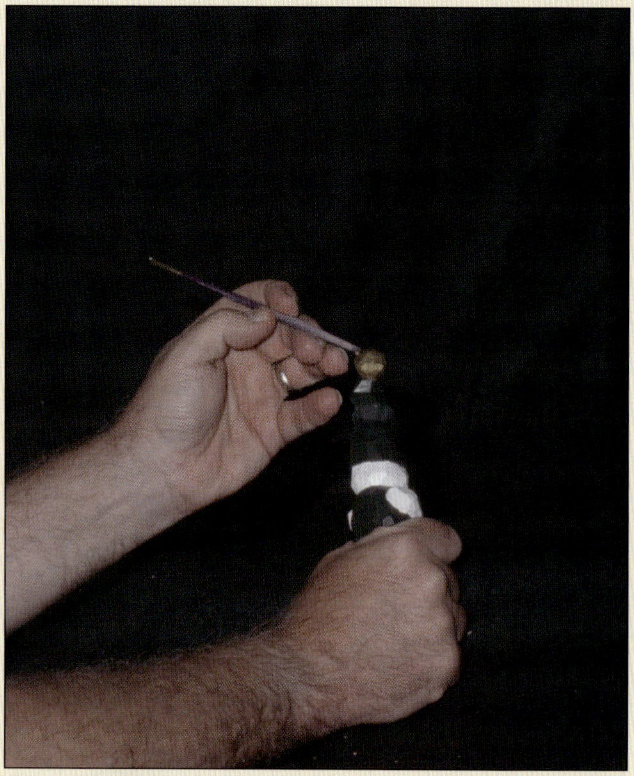

4 Paint the ball of the snowman's hat using metallic gold acrylic. Paint the tie with black cherry acrylic.

5 To paint the snowman's eyes, dip the tip of the paint brush handle in a small pool of black paint; then carefully touch the handle tip to the front of the snowman's head.

6 Dry brush the hat with metallic gold paint.

7 Place the painted snowman in the stand to dry.

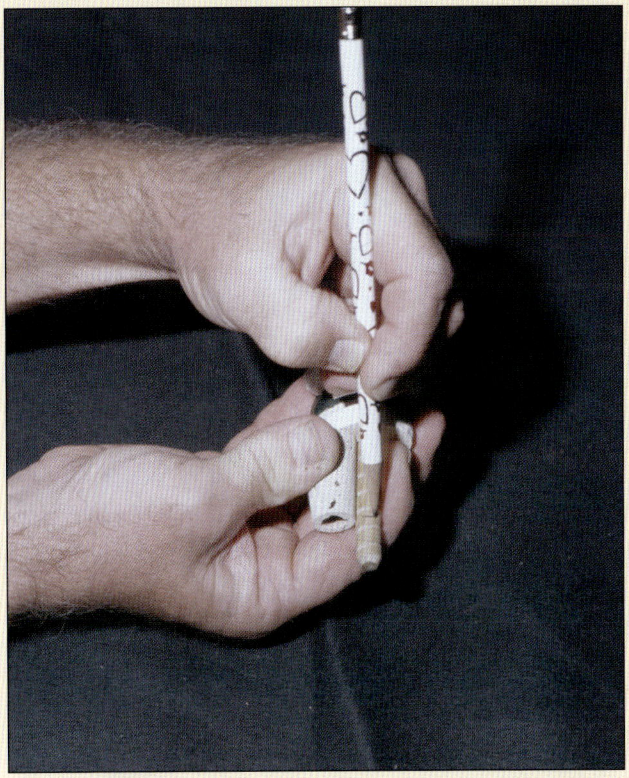

8 Glue the 3/8" hardwood dowel into the bottom of the snowman and mark the excess dowel to be cut off.

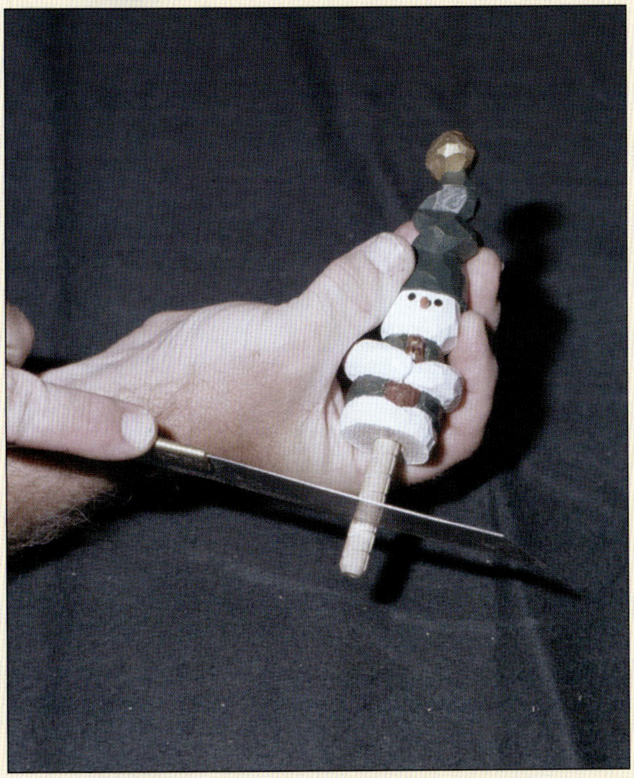

9 Using a small saw, cut off the excess dowel.

10 Glue the stopper in place.

Bow Tie Snowman

TOOLS

Bench knife
$\frac{1}{4}$" v-tool
$\frac{1}{8}$" v-tool
$\frac{1}{16}$" drill bit

MATERIALS

Wood to fit pattern
Round toothpick
22-gauge cloth wire
$\frac{3}{8}$" hardwood dowel
Pre-drilled cork stopper

QUICK TIP

As you begin to carve, be patient and take your time. Make clean, precise stop cuts and keep carving to those cuts until you have successfully removed the proper amount of waste wood.

Carving Tips: Round the corners of the snowman with a bench knife; then round the hat up to the ball on the top. With a pencil, draw lines between each snowball to separate them. Draw a line around the bottom of the hat as well. Using a $\frac{1}{4}$" v-tool, create stop cuts along the pencil lines. With a bench knife, carve both up to and then down to the stop cuts. Before shaping the hat any more, carefully round the ball on top of the snowman's hat.

With a pencil, draw a spiral up and around the hat. Use a $\frac{1}{4}$" v-tool to carve the spiral; then, using the bench knife, cut away wedges of wood around the spiral to exaggerate it.

Carve the bow tie separately. First draw lines on both sides of the knot. Then use the bench knife to create a shallow stop cut along these lines. Next, round and shape the top and sides of the bow tie. Use a $\frac{1}{8}$" v-tool to carve the creases in the bow tie. Attach the bow tie to the snowman by using some glue and a $\frac{1}{4}$" length of toothpick as a dowel.

Painting and Finishing Tips: When the paint has dried, load a stiff-bristled brush with metallic gold acrylic and dry brush the hat. This technique will add shimmering gold highlights to the blue hat. Glue the wire arms into place.

Body — White acrylic
Hat — Blueberry acrylic
Ball — Metallic gold acrylic
Bow Tie — Black cherry acrylic with blueberry acrylic dots
Nose — Orange acrylic
Buttons and Eyes — Black acrylic

NOVICE

PATTERN

Bunch of Grapes

TOOLS

7 mm #9 gouge
Bench knife
1/8" v-tool
5/8" #2 palm gouge
Woodburning pen (optional)

MATERIALS

Wood to fit pattern
3/8" hardwood dowel
Pre-drilled cork stopper

QUICK TIP

Use this quick tip to cut small repetitive pieces (such as the flowers in the basket of the bottle stopper on page 30). Cut the flower pattern from a thicker piece of wood, then mark lines along the side of this "flower log" and slice off thinner flower pieces, much like you slice cookies from a long roll of cookie dough.

Carving Tips: With a pencil, mark the thickness of the grape leaves at the back of the grape cluster. Use a bench knife to create a stop cut along these lines. On the front of the block, sketch in the outline of the cluster. Use the bench knife to create stop cuts along the lines where the grapes overlap the leaves. Remove the waste wood in front of the grape leaves and to the sides of the grape cluster with a bench knife or a 5/8" #2 palm gouge.

With a pencil, draw in the grapes. Next, use a 7 mm #9 gouge to shape the grapes. (The grapes do not need to match the pattern exactly to create a nice finished carving.) With the tip of the bench knife, clean out the cracks and crevices between the grapes.

Looking at the front of the cluster, use a pencil to mark the edge where the leaves overlap. Do the same on the back of the leaves. With a bench knife, create stop cuts along these lines. On the front of the cluster, use a 5/8" #2 palm gouge to remove wood from the recessed leaf. These cuts will lower that leaf and give the impression that the leaves are overlapping. Repeat this process on the back of the leaves. With a 1/8" v-tool or a woodburning pen, add the vein details on the fronts and backs of the leaves.

Painting Tips: Try adding a darker shade of purple where the grapes meet to give the illusion of shadows.

Grapes — Vintage wine acrylic
Leaves — Hunter green acrylic

NOVICE

PATTERN

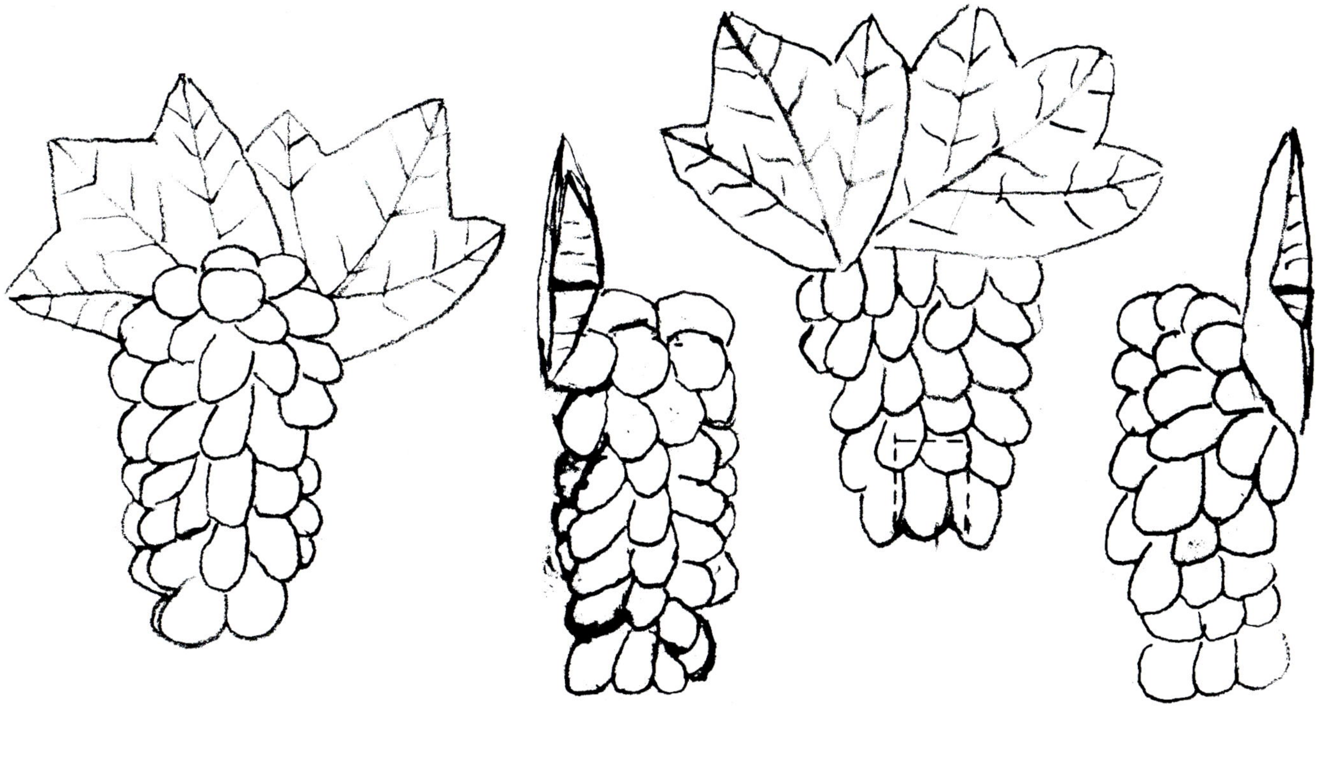

Halloween Ghost

TOOLS

Bench knife
10 mm #7 palm gouge
Rotary tool with very fine sanding drum
(or very fine sandpaper)

MATERIALS

Wood to fit pattern
3/8" hardwood dowel
Pre-drilled cork stopper

QUICK TIP

Dry brushing is a handy painting technique that will add interest to your finished project. Paint the base color as usual (eg: the block of the hat). Then load a stiff-bristled brush with a second color (eg: gold). Lightly brush across the figure to add highlights.

Carving Tips: Use a pencil to draw the brim lines of the hat on the sides of the block. Carefully use a bench knife to make a stop cut along the upper edge and the lower edge of the brim. Continuing to use the bench knife, begin to round and shape the ghost, being careful to carve with the grain. Try using a 10 mm #7 palm gouge to remove wood in some of the tighter spots, such as around the arms and in the curves of the body. Be especially careful when removing wood under the brim of the hat, as the wood is thin there and it can break rather easily. Round the corners of the top hat with the bench knife, being especially careful when carving down to the brim. Continuing to use the bench knife, round the brim of the hat. To pare down the thickness of the brim, work on the top of the brim and use the bench knife to carve from the outside edge of the brim in toward the top hat. Only the outside edge of the brim should be thin; make the brim thicker where the brim meets the "stovepipe" of the hat. To carve the underside of the brim, try using a 5/8" #2 palm gouge. Carve from the outside edge of the brim in toward the ghost's head. To carve the kinks in the hat stovepipe, use the bench knife to cut fairly large wedges from various sides of the hat. This makes the figure interesting and whimsical.

Painting Tips: After the paint dries, dry brush the top hat with metallic gold acrylic. To create the ghost's eyes, lightly spray the ghost with a clear acrylic matte sealer. Allow the sealer to dry; then use a fine point technical pen or fine point permanent marker to create the ovals for the eyes. Use black acrylic to paint the irises of both eyes. As a final touch, add a dot of white paint at the outside edges of both irises to make the eyes sparkle.

Body — White acrylic
Top hat — Black acrylic with metallic gold

NOVICE

PATTERN

Heart Stopper

TOOLS

Bench knife

MATERIALS

Wood to fit pattern
3/8" hardwood dowel
Pre-drilled cork stopper

QUICK TIP

To practice carving downhill with the grain, try carving egg-shaped or football-shaped objects from little blocks of basswood.

Carving Tips: After cutting out the blank, draw lines on both sides of the figure to separate the hearts. Make a stop cut along these lines, both front and back, with the tip of a bench knife.

Study the pattern closely before you begin carving. Notice that the bottom heart is larger and thicker than the two hearts above it. Starting with the smallest heart, use the bench knife to round and shape the edges of the heart; then carve away wood along the sides of the heart down to the stop cut. Repeat these steps with the middle heart. Finally, round the corners and edges of the bottom heart.

Painting Tips: After the hearts have dried, use a stiff paint brush loaded with metallic gold acrylic to dry brush the hearts.

Hearts—Bright red acrylic, metallic gold

NOVICE

PATTERN

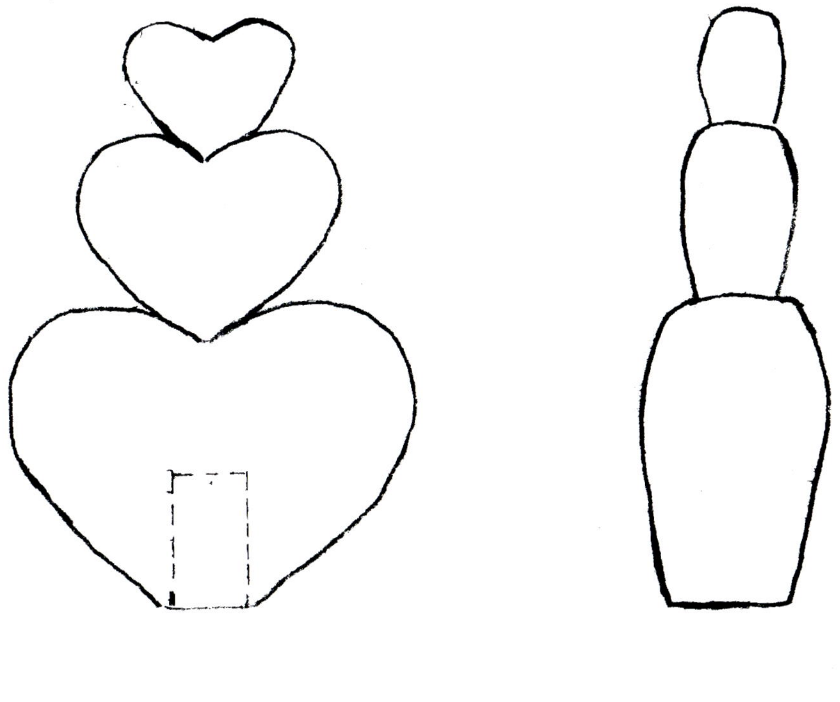

Hospitality Pineapple

TOOLS

Bench knife
¼" v-tool
10 mm #7 palm gouge
4 mm palm veiner

MATERIALS

Wood to fit the pattern
⅜" hardwood dowel
Pre-drilled cork stopper

QUICK TIP

Always drill the ⅜" hole in the bottom center of the block before you start carving. This will ensure that the hole is in the center; and drilling the hole when the carving is finished might cause the more fragile parts to break.

Carving Tips: Using a bench knife, round the corners of the pineapple. Start your cuts at the center of the body and carve both up and down, shaping the pineapple as you go. Carefully pencil in the crisscrossing lines around the pineapple. These crisscrossing lines should form a diamond pattern around the entire surface of the pineapple. Working with the grain, use a ¼" v-tool to carve the crisscrossing lines.

To create the leaves, first draw the leaves on the top part of the blank; then gently separate them using the bench knife. Continue to use the bench knife to establish stop cuts at the base on the top side of each leaf. On the top side of each leaf, use a 4 mm veiner to carve from the tip of the leaf to the stop cut at the leaf's base. This cut creates the concave surface of the leaf. On the bottom side of each leaf, use a 10 mm #7 palm gouge turned upside down. Starting at the leaf tip, carve the underside of the leaf from the tip to the base. This creates the convex shape on the bottom side of the leaf. Repeat these steps on each leaf.

Painting Tips: After the paint dries, use a stiff-bristled paint brush to dry brush the entire pineapple with metallic gold acrylic paint.

Pineapple — Brown acrylic
Leaves — Deep forest green acrylic

NOVICE

PATTERN

Pot of Gold

Carving Tips: Mark the center point on the top of the block of wood. Use a 1″ Forstner bit to hollow out the top of the pot. Drill down approximately ½".

Use a bench knife to round the outside of the pot to shape. (Note: You might find it easier to use a #7 palm gouge to create the concave surface around the perimeter of the pot.)

To carve the coins, mark thin lines along the length of a ⅜" dowel. Use a fine blade on a scroll saw or coping saw to cut the coins. Cut enough to fill the cavity in the pot. Sand the edges of the coins if needed. After the coins have been painted, glue the coins in place, a few at a time.

Painting Tips: When the black paint is dry, dry brush the outside of the pot with a stiff brush loaded with gold metallic acrylic paint.

Pot — Black acrylic and metallic gold

TOOLS

Bench knife
1" Forstner bit
#7 palm gouge (optional)

MATERIALS

Wood to fit pattern
⅜" hardwood dowel
Pre-drilled cork stopper

QUICK TIP

A gouge with a shape similar to that of the finished project can cut down on carving time and make a project easier. As an example, try a #3 or 5 palm gouge turned upside down to carve the outside of the pot to shape.

NOVICE

PATTERN

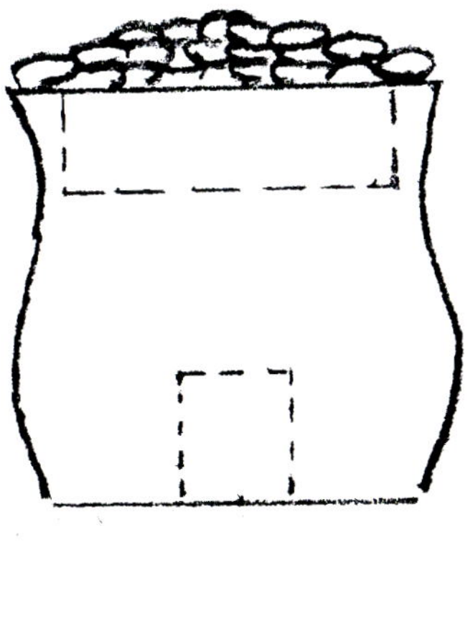

Basket of Flowers

TOOLS

Bench knife
5/8" #2 palm gouge
2 mm #11 mini gouge
4 mm #11 mini gouge
1/8" v-tool (or woodburning pen)
1/4" v-tool
10 mm #7 palm gouge
1/8" drill bit
1" Forstner drill bit
1/16" drill bit

MATERIALS

Wood to fit pattern
1/4" pieces of 1/8" hardwood dowel
Cloth-covered wire stems
3/8" hardwood dowel
Pre-drilled cork stopper

Carving Tips: Start with the body of the basket. Looking at the top of the basket, use a pencil to mark a line about 1/4" in from the outside edge of the basket. From the top outside edge of the basket, measure down 1/4" and draw a line around the entire circumference of the basket. Measure up 1/4" from the bottom edge of the basket and draw a line around the circumference of the basket.

With a 1" Forstner bit, hollow out the inside of the basket to the depth indicated on the pattern. Flatten the inside walls of the basket. Using a 1/4" v-tool, carve the lines that circle the sides of the basket. A 1/8" v-tool or woodburning pen is used to detail the lines along the top and bottom edge of the basket. To texture the mid portion of the basket, use a 2 mm #11 gouge to scoop out little cuts.

The handle is carved from a separate piece of basswood. First, drill a 1/8" hole in both ends of the basket handle and on the corresponding sides of the basket. Use the bench knife to round the handle, being careful to carve with the grain. Taper both bottom ends of the handle to fit the corresponding sides of the basket.

On a scrollsaw or bandsaw, cut out the flower part of the pattern. Mark the centers of the flowers with a pencil. Stop cut along this line with a 4 mm #11 mini gouge. Use a 10 mm #7 palm gouge to carve from the outside top edge of the flower to the stop cut at the center of the flower. This gives the face of the flower a subtle cupped look. Referring to the pattern, use a pencil to mark the lines separating and defining the petals. Carve these lines with a 1/8" v- tool. To further define the petals, cut little wedges between each petal with the bench knife.

Use a pin vise with a 1/16" drill bit to make the hole in the bottom of the flower where the stem is attached. Cut a cloth-covered wire stem to length, dab it in superglue, and stick the glued end into the base of the flower.

Assembly Tips: Paint the flowers and stain the basket first. Then drill 1/16" holes inside the basket. Dab the bottom tips of the flower stems in glue and stick the stems in the holes. Glue the 1/4" dowel pieces into the holes in the bottom of the handle; then glue the handle to the top of the basket.

Flower Petals — Yellow acrylic
Flower Centers — Black acrylic
Basket — Honey oak wood stain

BEGINNER

PATTERN

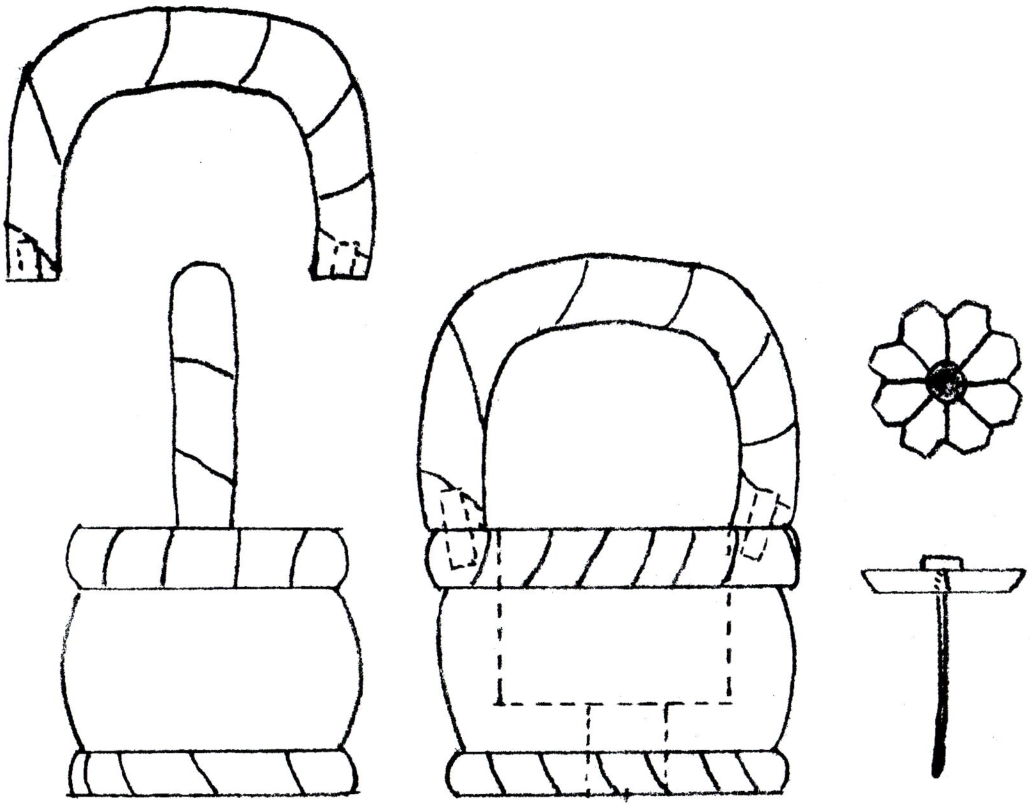

Christmas Tree

Carving Tips: Starting at the bottom of the Christmas tree cutout, use a bench knife to carve off the corners of the tree. Continue rounding the tree until it resembles a cone. Use the bench knife to create stop cuts in the corners of the tree trunk where the trunk meets the tree branches. Working from bottom to top, round the trunk using the bench knife.

Referring to the pattern, pencil in the boughs of the tree. The lines should roughly resemble three sets of large, interconnected W's encircling the tree. Establish a stop cut along all of lines. Starting at the bottom of the tree, use a 10 mm #7 palm gouge or its equivalent and carve up to the first set of stop cuts. Remove a bit more wood as you get closer to the stop cuts. Repeat this process in the middle section of the tree.

Starting at the bottoms of the boughs, use the ¼" v-tool to create gentle sweeping cuts in the bough sections. Always work from the bottom of the tree toward the top of the tree. Be sure to add a few cuts on the undersides of the branches, carving in toward the trunk. Use the v-tool and, if you have it, a wood burning pen to add texture lines to the trunk and the boughs.

Using the bench knife, carefully round the edges of the star. Drill a small, ⅛" hole between the points of the star. Check to make sure the star fits on the tree top; then glue it in place.

Painting Tips: Dry brush the entire tree with metallic gold acrylic after the tree is dry.

Tree — Forest green acrylic
Trunk — Burnt umber acrylic
Star — Metallic gold acrylic

TOOLS

Bench knife
10 mm #7 palm gouge
¼" v-tool
Woodburning pen (optional)
⅛" drill bit

MATERIALS

Wood to fit pattern
⅜" hardwood dowel
Pre-drilled cork stopper

QUICK TIP

When using a palm gouge, try carving away from your body as often as you can, being careful to keep the fingers holding the piece out of harm's way.

BEGINNER

PATTERN

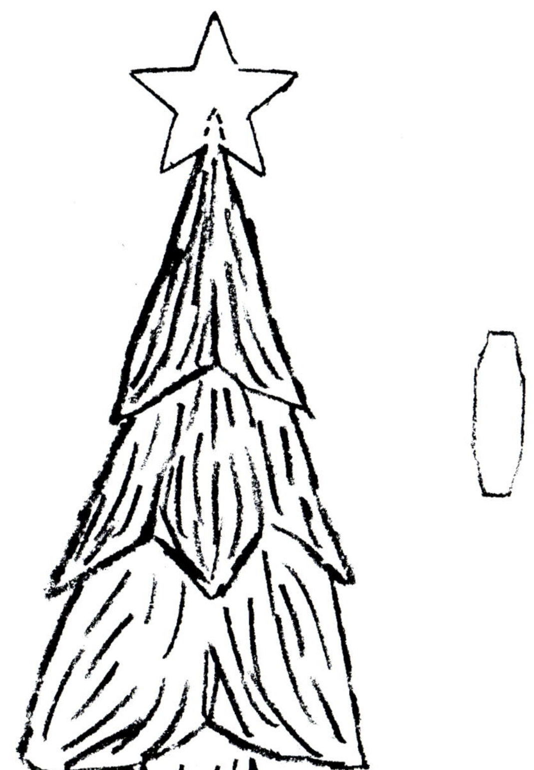

© Greg Young

Gentleman Jack-O'-Lantern

TOOLS

Bench knife
¼" v-tool
3 mm #3 gouge

MATERIALS

Wood to fit pattern
⅜" hardwood dowel
Pre-drilled cork stopper

QUICK TIP

Think carving a figure is too hard? Make it a bit easier by skipping the carved eye detail. Establish the brow ridge, then paint eye lines to make it look like the eyes are closed. (See the Leprechaun on page 54). Other tricks are to add a hat that covers the ears and most of the hair or to place the figure's hands in his pockets.

Carving Tips: Using a pencil, draw a centerline down the face and around the back of the pumpkin. Also draw a line around the bottom of the hat brim to distinguish the kinked top hat from the jack-o'-lantern's head.

With a bench knife, create a stop cut along the line that defines the bottom of the hat brim. Continuing to use the bench knife, carve off the corners of the pumpkin. Round the pumpkin up to the hat and down toward its base. With a pencil, draw the curved vertical lines on the pumpkin. Using the tip of the bench knife, cut a small stop cut just under the hat brim where the lobe lines meet the brim. Starting at the midpoint of the pumpkin, use a ¼" v-tool and carve the lobe lines up to the brim and then down under the pumpkin's base.

Pencil in triangles for the eyes, nose and mouth. These triangles will be cut by making chip carving cuts with the bench knife. First, create a stop cut along the lines defining the mouth with a bench knife. Then, using a small, shallow gouge (a 3 mm #3 works well), remove wood from inside the mouth.

Round, taper and better define the top of the brim with a bench knife. Continuing to use a bench knife, cut wedges out of the sides of the stovepipe portion of the hat to give it a kinked effect.

Painting Tips: When dry, brush the entire piece with metallic gold acrylic.

Pumpkin — Orange acrylic
Eyes, Nose and Mouth — Black acrylic
Hat — Black with orange acrylic triangles

BEGINNER

PATTERN

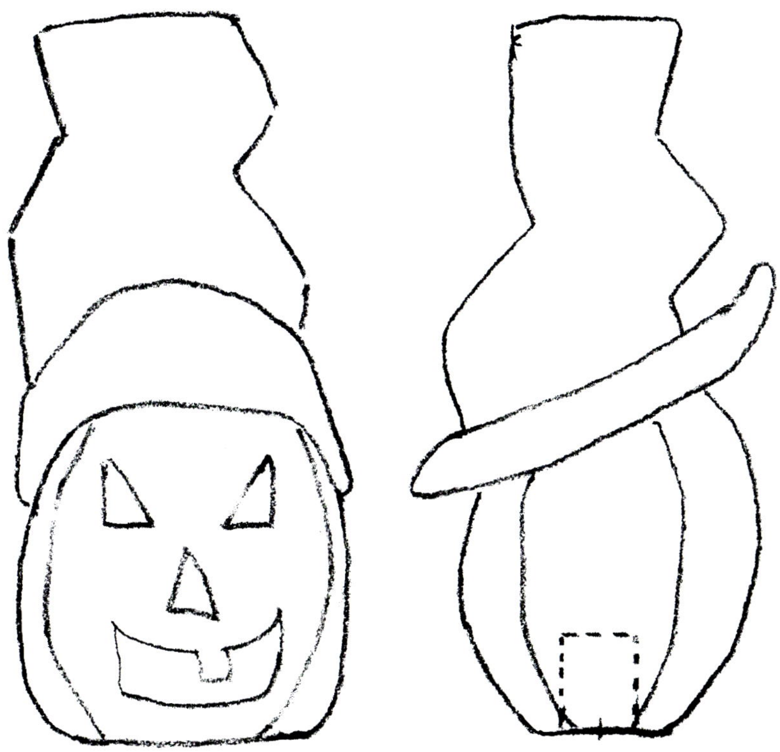

© Greg Young

Liberty Bell

Carving Tips: With a pencil, draw lines on the top of the bell beam to indicate the thickness of the beam. Draw a line on both sides of the bell to indicate where the bell joins the beam. Using a bench knife, create stop cuts along these lines. Continuing to use the bench knife, remove the waste wood from the outside faces of the bell beam until the desired thickness of the beam is achieved.

Begin to round and taper the outside of the bell, always carving from the bottom of the bell up to the beam. Mark the width lines for the clapper on the bottom center of the bell and then carefully round the clapper.

Use a woodburning pen to texture the beam. Burn the crack on the outside of the Liberty Bell with the woodburning pen or carve the crack with a small 1-2 mm palm v-tool.

Mark and drill the ⅛" holes and the 3⁄16" hole on the top of the beam. Glue and insert the dowel pieces. Allow the glue to dry; then carve the tops of the dowel pieces until they are rounded and about the same height.

Painting Tips: A good quality metallic bronze acrylic paint will give the finished bell an authentic look.

Beam — Driftwood or blue smoke acrylic
Bell — Metallic bronze acrylic

TOOLS

Bench knife
1-2 mm palm v-tool (or woodburning pen)
⅛" and 3⁄16" drill bits

MATERIALS

8 pieces of ⅛" dowel approximately ¼" in length
1 piece of 3⁄16" dowel approximately ¼" in length
⅜" hardwood dowel
Pre-drilled cork stopper

QUICK TIP

When the wood of the project you are working on is soft or crumbly, try using a woodburning pen to create detail.

PATTERN

BEGINNER

© Greg Young

Mouse

TOOLS

Bench knife
1/8" v-tool
5 mm #11 palm gouge
10 mm #7 palm gouge
Rotary carving tool and flame-shaped ruby carving bit

MATERIALS

Thumbtack
(2) 3 mm black plastic beads for eyes
6 pieces of synthetic bristle from an old or very inexpensive paintbrush
3/8" hardwood dowel
Pre-drilled cork stopper

Carving Tips: With a pencil, draw a centerline the length of the mouse's body, over his head, nose, and chest, and down his tail. Referring to the pattern, sketch the contours of the body, tail and head. Using a bench knife, care-fully carve both sides of the mouse; narrow the tail, taper the head, and shape the body.

Referring to the top view pattern, use a pencil to draw the arc lines that define the backs of the mouse's ears. Remove the waste wood from between the ears with a 10 mm #7 palm gouge until the area between the ears blends with the rest of the head. Shape the backs of the ears. On the fronts of the ears, pencil in lines just inside the outer edges of the outside of the ear. With a 1/8" v-tool, create a stop cut along these lines. Using a 5 mm #11 gouge remove a bit of waste wood to make the inner ears concave.

Referring to the side view pattern, sketch in the rear leg lines; then, with the bench knife, create stop cuts along these lines. Remove some of the waste wood from between the legs. Repeat this process on the other side of the mouse as well.

Referring to the front view pattern, sketch the lines that define the mouse's overhanging front legs. With the bench knife, create a stop cut along these lines. Continuing to use the bench knife, remove waste wood from between the front legs and round the legs. With a pencil, draw the toe lines on the tips of the front paws. Use a 1/8" v-tool to carve the toe lines.

Looking at the mouse's face, sketch in the nose and carve those lines with the 1/8" v-tool. Draw faint pencil lines from the left top edge and the right top edge of its nose to each corre-sponding ear. Using a 5 mm #11 palm gouge, scoop out a little portion of wood along each of these lines. With a pencil, carefully mark an "x" in the mid-part of these hollowed-out areas. Use a rotary carving tool fitted with a flame-shaped ruby carving bit to carve a hole directly into each "x." These holes should be just large enough to seat the black plastic beads.

Finishing Tips: Use the bristles from an old paint brush to create whiskers. Referring to the pattern, use a pencil to mark three dots on each side of the nose. With a thumbtack or pushpin, poke small holes in each of the dots. Dip one bristle in a little glue and insert it into one hole. Repeat this process with the other whiskers. Glue the black bead eyes into the eye sockets.

Body — Light gray acrylic
Inside of Ears — Deep portrait pink acrylic
Nose — Black acrylic

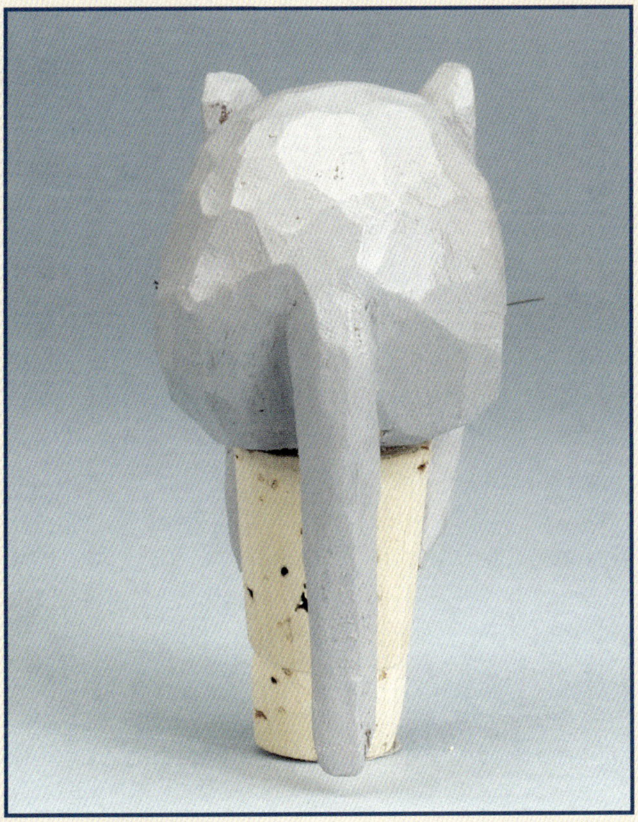

BEGINNER

PATTERN

Chilly Penguin

Use a pencil to draw the top and bottom brim lines around the hat. Also draw the bottom of the ball on the top of the hat. With a 1/4" v-tool, carve along the lines that you have just drawn. Use a bench knife to round the body of the penguin. Do not carve the flippers, beak or feet during this step.) Still using the bench knife, round the penguin's hat. Make sure to repeat the stop cuts and remove the material around the brim to make the brim stand out.

Referring to the pattern, draw the penguin's flippers and feet. Use the 1/4" v-tool to carve the flipper lines and the tops and sides of the penguin's feet. Use the bench knife to remove waste wood from around the feet. Continue rounding and shaping the beak with the bench knife. Drill a 1/16" hole in the penguin's chest to accept the bow tie.

The bow tie is carved separately. First, draw a line around the knot; then create stop cuts along knot lines. Carve toward the stop cuts, shaping the bow and the knot. With a 1/8" v-tool, carve the creases in the tie and the toes on each foot. Also use the same v-tool to carve the vertical ribbing on the brim of the hat.

TOOLS

Bench knife
1/4" v-tool
1/8" v-tool
1/16" drill bit

MATERIALS

1/4" long piece of a round toothpick
3/8" hardwood dowel
Pre-drilled cork stopper

Carving Tips: Referring to the pattern, use a pencil to mark the location of the bow tie. Using a drill fitted with a 1/16" drill bit, drill a hole in the penguin and a shallow hole in the back of the bow tie.

Painting and Finishing Tips: Dry brush the hat and black areas with metallic gold acrylic. Try using the handle of a paintbrush to create the large eyes. Glue the 1/4" piece of toothpick into the hole on the back of the bow tie. Allow the glue to dry, then insert the bow tie into the hole in the penguin's chest.

Breast and Eyes — White acrylic
Feet, Flippers, Beak and Back — Black acrylic
Hat — Blue acrylic
Bow Tie — Black cherry acrylic

BEGINNER

PATTERN

© Greg Young

Nesting Robin

Carving Tips: Using a pencil, draw the top edge of the nest; then draw a centerline through the length of the robin. Sketch in the contours of the tail, body, head and beak. With a bench knife, create stop cuts following the pencil lines that mark the edge of the nest. Use the bench knife to remove waste wood from the sides of the robin down to the top of the nest. Continue to round and shape the robin and the nest with the bench knife.

To make the robin smooth, use a rotary tool with a very fine sandpaper drum or very fine sandpaper. Draw pencil lines to define the wings, tail feathers and a few feathers on each wing; carve the lines with a 1/8" v-tool. Use the bench knife to further separate the wing tips from the tail.

Texture the nest with the 1/8" v-tool. Use a woodburning pen to supplement the 1/8" v-tool cuts.

Painting Tips: For the robin's orange breast, mix soft white acrylic with orange acrylic to make a softer color.

Nest — Honey oak wood stain
Wings, Tail and Head — Black acrylic
Beak — Yellow acrylic
Eyes and Throat — White acrylic
Breast — Soft white and orange acrylic mix

TOOLS

Bench knife
1/8" v-tool
Rotary tool with a very fine sanding drum or very fine sandpaper
Woodburning pen (optional)

MATERIALS

Wood to fit pattern
3/8" hardwood dowel
Pre-drilled cork stopper

QUICK TIP

Give eyes a more lifelike appearance by adding a tiny dot of white in each pupil. Use a round object, such as a toothpick or a small finishing nail, to dab the white paint in the upper left (or upper right) of the pupil.

BEGINNER

PATTERN

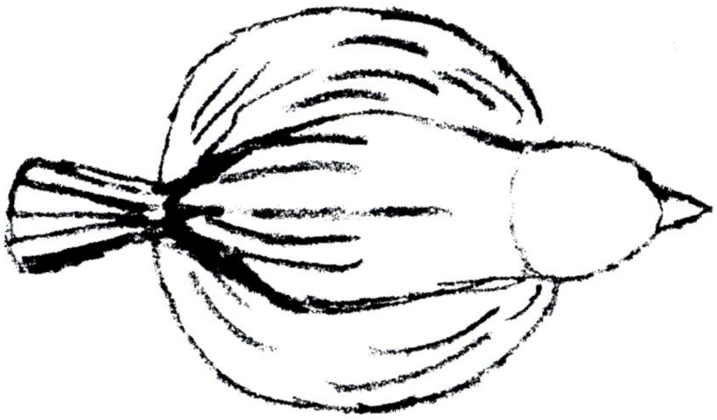

Oak Barrel

Carving Tips: Before you start to carve the barrel, mark the center of each end of the block of wood and transfer the end pattern to the wood block. Then use a 1" Forstner drill bit to recess both ends of the block of wood to about 1/8" deep. With a 3/8" drill bit, drill a hole in the bottom of the barrel to accommodate the dowel.

Starting on the top at the center of the block of wood, work toward the end of the block and carve off the corners. Continue to carve all around the block of wood until you get a general barrel shape.

Mark the bands that encircle the barrel; carve them using a v-tool.

Draw lines lengthwise to mark the slats of the barrel, and carve them all around the barrel. NOTE: Always start in the middle, at the high point of the barrel, and carve "downhill" toward each end.

Mark and drill a 3/16" hole for the barrel tap. Carve the small tap using a bench knife.

Painting and Finishing Tips: Paint the barrel bands and tap a dark brown acrylic. Use a honey oak wood stain or a light acrylic wash of a similar color for the barrel. Glue the barrel tap into the barrel end using super glue.

Barrel — Honey oak wood stain

Barrel Bands and Tap — Dark brown acrylic

TOOLS

Bench knife
1/4" palm v-tool,
3/16" drill bit
1" Forstner bit

MATERIALS

2 pieces of basswood, one small,
Thin piece for use as barrel tap, the other for barrel
3/8" hardwood dowel
Pre-drilled cork stopper

QUICK TIP

Be sure that the grain runs lengthwise through this project. Try drawing a few lines or arrows on your project to remind you of the general grain direction.

BEGINNER

PATTERN

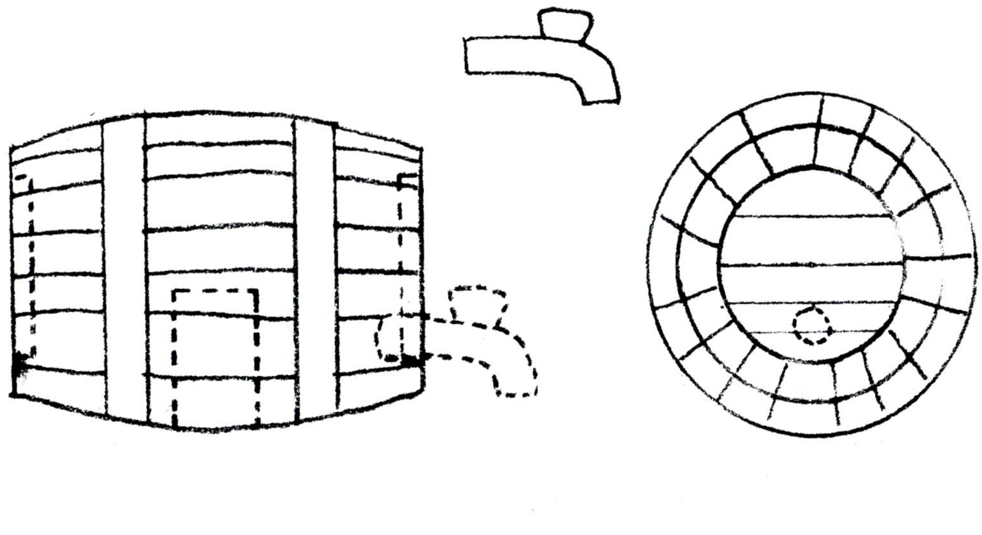

© Greg Young

Rose-Breasted Nuthatch on Acorn

TOOLS

Bench knife
¼" v-tool
⅛" v-tool
Woodburning pen (optional)

MATERIALS

Wood to fit pattern
⅜" hardwood dowel
Pre-drilled cork stopper

Carving Tips: With a pencil, draw a centerline on the top of the nuthatch and around the length of the acorn. Draw a line at the bottom of the nuthatch where the bird comes into contact with the acorn. Looking down at the top of the nuthatch, sketch the contours of the tail, body and head.

Using a bench knife, establish a stop cut along the line that separates the nuthatch from the acorn. Then, starting at the breast and throat area of the nuthatch, carve down to the stop cut to round and better define the underside of the bird. Next, use the bench knife to taper and shape the body, tail, head and beak.

Mark the wings on the side of the nuthatch's body with a pencil. Draw in a few feather detail lines on the wings and the tail. Carving in the direction of the grain, use the ¼" v-tool to carve along the lines that separate the wings from the tail. Then, using the bench knife, carefully carve away just enough wood under the wings to blend and further separate the wings from the sides of the bird's body. Carve the wing and tail feather lines with the ⅛" v-tool or burn them with a woodburning tool.

Round the corners of the acorn with a bench knife, being careful to carve with the grain. Draw a pencil line around the acorn to separate the cap from the acorn's body. Carve this line with a ¼" v-tool. Take your bench knife and carve from the body of the acorn to the cap. Continue this all around the acorn (at least where a nuthatch isn't perched!). With a bench knife, carve stop cuts in the acorn cap where the stem joins the cap. Gently carve away the waste wood to shape the stem. Draw the crisscross pattern on the cap with a pencil; then carve those lines with the ¼" v-tool.

Painting Tips: Dab a small round object, such as a toothpick or the end of a paint brush, in black acrylic to dot the eyes. Add a tiny dot of white acrylic to give them a "spark."

Acorn — Bambi brown and burnt umber acrylic
Wings and Tail — Sky blue acrylic
Throat, Breast and Underside — Santa Fe rose acrylic
Sides of Head —White acrylic
Cap and Stripes on Head — Black acrylic

BEGINNER

PATTERN

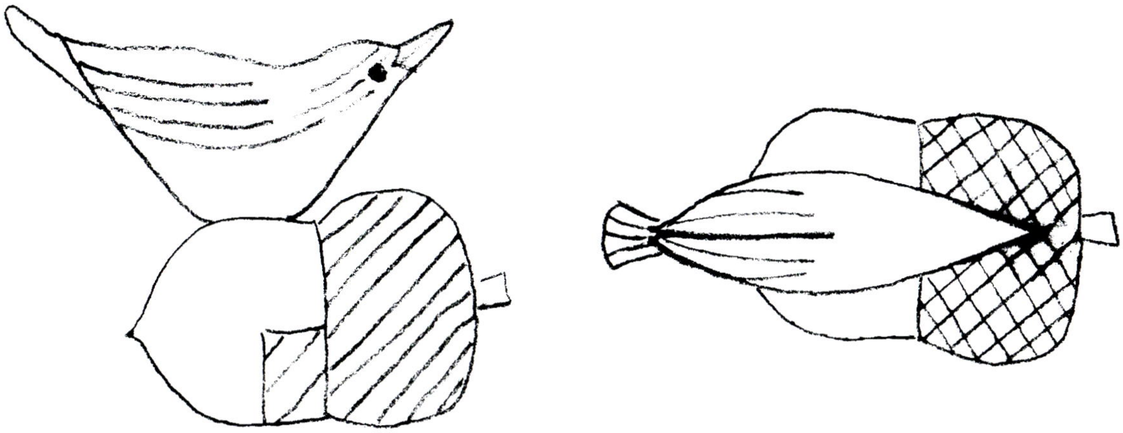

© Greg Young

Toad on a Toadstool

TOOLS

Bench knife
1/8" v-tool
1/4" v-tool
5 mm #11 palm gouge
Rotary carving tool with a fine flame-shaped ruby bit
1/16" drill bit

MATERIALS

Wood to fit pattern
(2) 5 mm black plastic beads
3/8" hardwood dowel
Pre-drilled cork stopper

Carving Tips: Using a pencil, sketch the bottom of the toad where it comes in contact with the toadstool. Looking at the side view, sketch the front leg and rear leg on the cutout. Looking at the front view, sketch the arms.

With a 1/4" v-tool, carve the lines that separate the toad from the toadstool. Continuing with the v-tool, remove wood from under the toad's front feet; then carve the lines that distinguish the toad legs. Use a bench knife to create a stop cut along the inside of the front legs next to the toad belly. Create another stop cut along the toad belly where the belly comes in contact with the toadstool. Cut small wedges, working both up and down, to define and separate the front legs from the belly. Carve away a small amount of wood where the front legs cross over the rear legs.

Fit a rotary carving tool with a flame-shaped ruby bit; then round and smooth the body of the toad. To distinguish the muscle mass for the rear legs, pencil in a line that arcs over the rear legs and ends just outside the center tail bone. Carve this line using either the rotary tool with a flame-shaped ruby bit or a 5 mm #11 gouge.

Use a pencil to mark the eye sockets; then draw an arc on the top of the head just behind each eye. Using a rotary tool fitted with a flame-shaped ruby bit, remove some of the wood along the arcs on top of the head, as well as some wood from the center and front of the top of the head. This creates the prominent bulging eye "bumps." Still using the rotary tool, carve directly into the sides of the toad's head until you have an eye socket about 5 mm in diameter. Draw the toad's mouth line. Using a 1/8" v-tool, carve the mouth line as well as the center line that runs down the back. Mark the toad's nostrils and drill them with a 1/16" drill bit.

To carve the toadstool, use a bench knife to round the top and the outside edge of the toadstool, giving it a "domed" look. Use the bench knife to round the stem of the toadstool. To carve the underside of the toadstool's cap, use a 1/4" v-tool to create lines that look like spokes radiating out from the stem to the edge of the toadstool's cap.

To finish, pencil in lines on the front feet that separate the toes. Carve these lines and define the toes with a 1/4" v-tool.

Painting Tips: After the paint dries, glue the beads into the eye sockets.

Body — Light gray acrylic, storm gray spots
Chest and Stripe — Soft white acrylic
Toadstool Cap — Bambi brown acrylic
with red oxide acrylic dots
Stem and Underside — Antique white acrylic

BEGINNER

PATTERN

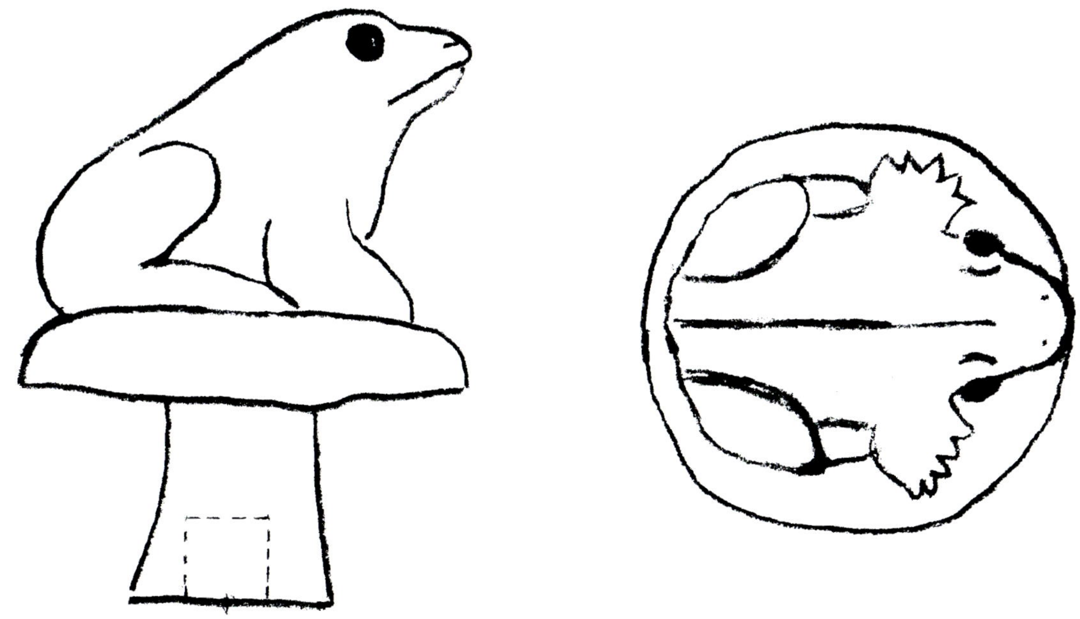

Valentine Bear

TOOLS

Bench knife
1/4" v-tool
1/8" v-tool
5 mm #11 gouge
3 mm #9 gouge
3 mm #5 palm gouge
Woodburning pen (optional)

MATERIALS

Wood to fit pattern
3/8" hardwood dowel
Pre-drilled cork stopper

Carving Tips: Using the pattern as reference, draw in the following details. On the side view of the block, draw in pencil lines to show where the back of the heart meets the teddy bear's chest. Next, sketch the front paws holding onto the sides of the heart. On the front of the block, draw a centerline over the bear's head, nose, heart and lower body. Sketch the shape of the heart, the feet, and the ears. Draw the centerline down his back as well. Turn the block upside down and draw the insides of the bear's bottom legs.

Starting on a side view, use the bench knife to create stop cuts along the top and bottom of the bear's arm. Carve away waste wood from above and below the arm. Continuing with the bench knife, carefully create stop cuts along the lines that outline the bear's paws on the heart; then remove some of the waste wood. Next, create stop cuts along the lines of the heart; then remove waste wood around the heart to shape it. Repeat these steps to form the heart.

With the bench knife, create stop cuts along the lines that indicate the top of the bear's lower legs and along the inside leg lines on the bottom of the figure. Using the bench knife, shape the bear's legs and feet. A 3mm #5 palm gouge works well in the tight spots between the legs and the lower parts of the heart.

Create stop cuts along the lines of the ears; then carve away the waste wood around the ears. Laying the bench knife flat against the top of the bear's head, use the tip to create a stop cut along the front inside base of each ear. Starting just inside the top of each ear, use a 5 mm #11 gouge to hollow out the fronts of the ears.

Use the bench knife to shape the bear's muzzle, head, and backs of the ears. Continue to use the bench knife to give final shape to the bear's back, arms and legs. Use your pencil to draw the eyes, nose, mouth and toes, and to redraw the centerline on the front of the head. Carve the features with a 1/8" v-tool.

To carve the bear's eyes, use the 3 mm #9 gouge to create stop cuts along the penciled-in circles. Then, laying the bench knife nearly flat along the bear's face, carve away tiny shavings of wood from the center of each eye out to the stop cut.

Texture the fur of the bear with a 1/8" v-tool or a woodburning pen.

Painting Tips: Try painting the eyes instead of carving them. Use white for the eyeball, a color for the iris, and black for the pupil. Add a tiny white highlight to the pupil with a toothpick.

Body — Burnt umber acrylic
Heart — Tompte red acrylic
Eyes, Inside Ears —Black acrylic

PATTERN

BEGINNER

© Greg Young

Cornucopia

TOOLS

Bench knife
¼" v-tool
⅛" v-tool
3 mm #11 gouge
1" Forstner bit
Rotary carving tool with flame-shaped carbide burr and flame-shaped ruby carving bit

MATERIALS

Wood to fit pattern
16-gauge cloth wire
⅜" hardwood dowel
Pre-drilled cork stopper

Carving Tips: Find a rectangular piece of wood to fit the pattern. Draw the profile of the cornucopia pattern on the side of the block with a pencil. Mark the center of the end of the block where the mouth of the cornucopia is located. Referring to the pattern, drill a hole approximately 1" deep with a 1" Forstner bit. Widen and taper the hole with a rotary carver fitted with a flame-shaped carbide bit. Switch to a flame-tipped ruby carving bit and smooth the inside of the cornucopia.

On the outside of the cornucopia, pencil in a line for the reinforced woven band at the mouth of the cornucopia. Carve this line using a ¼" v-tool. To further detail it, use a ⅛" v-tool to create the wraps around the band. Texture the cornucopia with a 3 mm #11 gouge by making small scooping cuts around the cornucopia.

The food inside the cornucopia is carved separately. To carve ears of corn, mark one end for the stem and draw lines lengthwise and widthwise around the ear to define the kernels. Carve the kernels with the ⅛" v-tool. To carve the apple and pear, use a bench knife to round and shape each fruit. To carve the pumpkin, draw the stem and remove the waste wood from around the stem with a bench knife. Be sure to create stop cuts alongside the stem before carving away the waste wood. Round and shape the pumpkin; then use a pencil to draw in the curved vertical lobe lines around the pumpkin. Carve these lines with a ¼" v-tool.

Note: To carve the small fruits, I find it easier to shape them on a stick. Simply carve the end of a piece of wood to the appropriate shape (e.g. an apple). Then cut through the stick as you make your final cuts. The stick acts as a mini-holder.

Finishing Tips: Position the ears of corn and pumpkin and glue them in place at their contact points with each other and with the sides of the cornucopia. Stems may also be created from ¼" pieces of cloth wire. Drill holes in the fruit then glue the wire into place. Then glue the fruit.

Corn — Empire gold acrylic
Pear — Empire gold dry-brushed with red acrylic
Apple — Red acrylic
Pumpkin — Orange acrylic
Stems — Green acrylic
Cornucopia — Honey oak wood stain

PATTERN

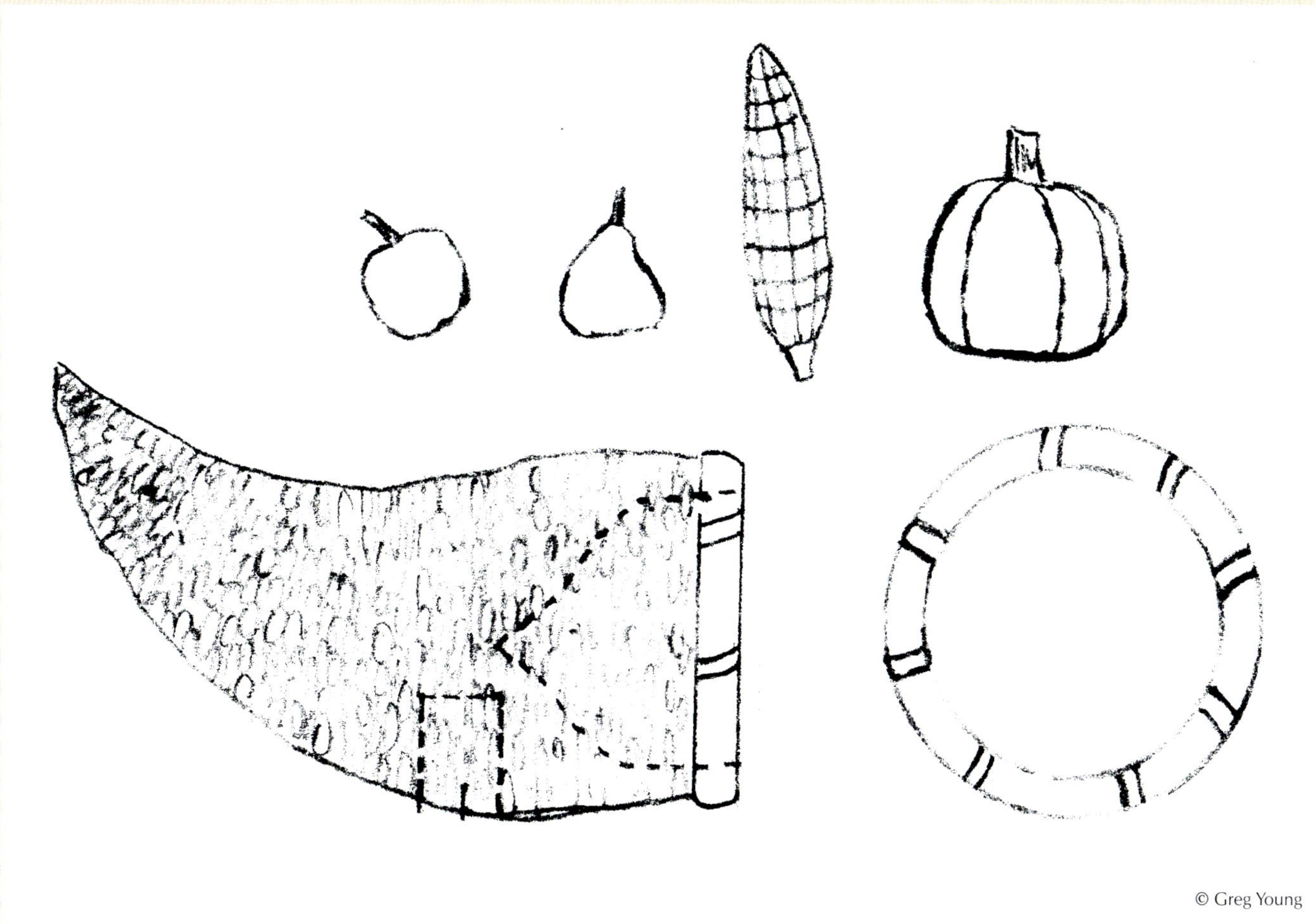

© Greg Young

INTERMEDIATE

The Leprechaun

TOOLS

Bench knife
Coping saw
1/4" v-tool
1/8" v-tool
10 mm #7 gouge
5/8" #2 palm gouge
5 mm #11 gouge
1/16" drill bit
Woodburning pen (optional)

MATERIALS

Wood to fit pattern
3/8" hardwood dowel
Pre-drilled cork stopper

Carving Tips: Use the side view pattern to make the blank for this piece. With a pencil, draw a centerline vertically through the Leprechaun's face, beard, hat, and head. Draw a line around the bottom of the hat. Draw the upper brim line of the hat on both sides of the block. Carefully use a coping saw to make stop cuts along the upper and lower lines that define the hat brim.

Using a bench knife, remove waste wood from under the hat to shape the head. Be especially careful removing wood up to the brim of the hat. Carve the sides of the hat down to the stop cut around the top of the brim. Round the edge of the brim. Pare down brim—start on the top of the brim and carve from the outside edge in to the hat. To carve the underside of the brim, use a 5/8" #2 palm gouge. Remember to always carve from the outside edge of the brim in toward the head.

Round the sides of the hat. Draw in the band and buckle at the base of the hat. With a 1/4" v-tool, carve the outside of the buckle. To carve the little window inside the buckle, first create a stop cut with the bench knife along the inner buckle lines. Then use a 3 mm #3 palm gouge to carve a little wood from within the buckle window.

Pencil in the ears and sideburns. With the 1/4" v-tool, carve along the outside ear lines; then carve along both sides and the bottom of each sideburn. Using a 10 mm #7 palm gouge, carve a deeper stop cut in the v-tool cuts around the back of the ear. Angle the gouge slightly so that it undercuts the backside of the ear. Use the bench knife to remove the wood behind the ear. To carve and hollow the inner portion of the ear, use a 5 mm #11 gouge to create a stop cut along the inner ear line. Remove wood up to the sideburn. With the bench knife, carve away the v-tool marks on the facial side of the sideburn.

Draw the collar lines on the leprechaun's neck; then use the 1/4" v-tool to carve the collar lines. Use the bench knife to remove the wood below the collar. To carve the shamrock tie, first use a 1/16" drill bit to drill a shallow hole in the back of the shamrock. Still using this drill bit, drill the hole just under his collar for the shamrock tie. Use your bench knife to round the edges of the shamrock; then glue a 1/4" piece of toothpick into the back of the shamrock tie.

See the instructions on page 60 for carving lips.

Painting Tips:

Hat and Tie — Hunter green acrylic
Face — Deep portrait pink acrylic
Collar — White acrylic
Hat Band — Black acrylic
Buckle — Metallic gold acrylic
Beard — Red oxide acrylic

PATTERN

INTERMEDIATE

Lighthouse

TOOLS

1/4" v-tool
1/8" v-tool
3 mm #3 gouge
10 mm #7 gouge
1" Forstner drill bit
1/8" drill bit
Woodburning pen (optional)

MATERIALS

Wood to fit pattern
1/4" piece of 1/8" hardwood dowel
3/8" hardwood dowel
Pre-drilled cork stopper

Carving Tips: The light housing is a separate piece, so you'll need to carve the lighthouse tower first. Mark the center of the top of the tower with a pencil. Using a 1" Forstner bit, drill down to the depth indicated on the pattern. Switch to the 1/8″ drill bit and drill a hole in the center of the recessed area. Also drill a 1/8" hole in the bottom center of the lighthouse. Then, using a bench knife, round the corners of the blank. Continue rounding and shaping until the lighthouse tower is nicely rounded. When shaping the top, overhanging part of the tower, be sure to carve from the top edge of the lighthouse down to the narrow area on the lighthouse. Use a 10 mm #7 gouge to blend the areas together.

Using a pencil to draw lines for the stones, windows and door. Carve the stones with a 1/4" v-tool. Tip: Using a woodburning pen to burn lines between the stones after carving them enhances their depth. Use a bench knife to create stop cuts for the door and the two windows. Switch to a 3 mm #3 gouge and remove the waste wood from the windows and the door.

To carve the light housing, first use a pencil to draw a line defining the bottom of the overhanging roof. Cut a stop cut along this line with a bench knife. Continuing to use the bench knife, round the sides of the light housing up to the overhanging roof and down to its bottom edge. Draw the thin vertical window frame pieces with a pencil. Carve these lines with a 1/8" v-tool. Use the bench knife to blend the windows where they meet the vertical frames. Pencil in the shingle lines on the roof and carve them with a 1/8" v-tool or a woodburning pen.

Glue the 1/4" piece of 1/8" hardwood dowel into the bottom of the light housing. Glue the housing firmly in place on top of the tower.

Painting Tips: Dry brush the painted stone tower with a light gray acrylic.

Stones — Storm gray acrylic
Windows, Door and Frames — Black acrylic
Light Housing Windows — White acrylic
Roof — Black cherry acrylic

PATTERN

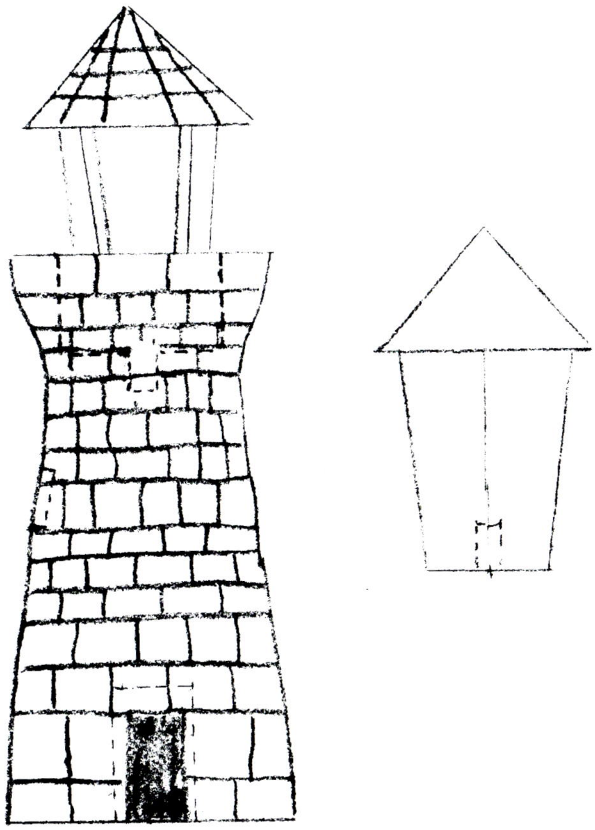

© Greg Young

INTERMEDIATE

Uncle Sam

Carving Tips: To carve the hat, use a pencil to draw the brim lines of the hat on both sides of the hat. (This assumes that your cutout is sawn using the side view pattern). Carefully use a coping saw to make stop cuts along the upper and lower lines that you have drawn to define the hat brim. With a bench knife, remove waste wood from under the hat, shaping the head. (Please note: Be especially careful in removing wood up to the brim of the hat as it can break rather easily). With the bench knife, carve the sides of the stovepipe down to the stop-cut around the top of the brim. Continuing with the bench knife, round the edge of the brim. To pare down the thickness of the brim, starting on the top of the brim, use the bench knife to carve from the outside edge of the brim in to the stovepipe of the hat. Carve just the outside edge. To carve the underside of the brim, I find that using the 5/8" #2 palm gouge works well. Just be sure to always carve from the outside edge of the brim in toward the head. To carve the kinks in the hat stovepipe, use your bench knife to cut fairly large wedges from various sides of the hat.

Refer to the Santa Stopper on page 64 for instructions on carving a face.

Painting Tips: Before you paint Uncle Sam's hat, refer to the pictures, and then use your pencil to lightly draw the vertical stripes and horizontal stripe. Wait until the paint has dried completely before adding the stars around the hat. Paint the hair, beard and eyebrows with a base color of storm gray and a top color of soft white.

Hat — Tompte red, navy blue and soft white acrylic

Hair, Beard and Eyebrows — Storm gray and soft white acrylic

Face — Deep portrait pink acrylic

Eyes — Blueberry acrylic iris with black pupil

TOOLS

Bench knife
1/4" v-tool
1/8" v-tool
5/8" #2 gouge
10 mm #7 gouge
Coping saw
Woodburning pen (optional)

MATERIALS

Wood to fit pattern
3/8" hardwood dowel
Pre-drilled cork stopper

QUICK TIP

To texture hair, try using a few different sized v-tools and a woodburning pen. Doing this creates an interesting variation in hair texture.

PATTERN

© Greg Young

INTERMEDIATE

The Viking

TOOLS

Bench knife
1/4" v-tool
1/8" v-tool
10 mm #7 gouge
Woodburning pen (optional)

MATERIALS

Wood to fit pattern
3/8" hardwood dowel
Pre-drilled cork stopper

Carving Tips: Using a pencil, draw a centerline on the Viking's face. Start at the bottom of the beard, continue over the top of his hat, and then down the back of his head. Draw a line around the bottom of the hat to separate it from the Viking's head.

Round the corners of the figure with a bench knife. Draw the horns on the Viking's helmet. Cut stop cuts along those lines with a bench knife; then carve away the waste wood. Note: The horns are prone to breakage. Be careful not to apply too much pressure as you carve.

After rounding the horns, use a pencil to draw in the bands that go around and over the Viking's helmet. Study the pictures of the finished Viking carefully. Notice how the band that goes from front to back over the top of his helmet lays over the band going from horn to horn over the top.

Using a 1/4" v-tool, carve the line defining the top of the horizontal band that goes around his head. Carve the front-to-back band lines first. Use your bench knife to remove a small amount of wood from both sides of the band, making it stand out. Redraw the portion of the horn-to-horn band lines that you carved away. Use the 1/4" v-tool to carve these lines; then use a bench knife to remove a small amount of wood from both sides of the band. Remember that you are only carving the horn-to-horn band, not the front-to-back band in this step.

To carve the Viking's lower lip, first draw the inside lines of his moustache. Where the two inside lines meet, they form an inverted "v." Use the tip of the bench knife to make a small chip carving cut along these lines. Draw in the lower lip lines about 1/3" below the inverted "v." Make a chip carving cut along the top line of the lower lip. Use the tip of your bench knife to make a small chip carving cut along the lines forming the inside of the moustache, and along the top of the lower lip. Use a 1/8" v-tool to carve the bottom lower lip line. Round the lip with a bench knife, removing a small amount of wood where the lips contact the inside edges of the moustache.

Painting Tips: To give the Viking a Nordic look, mix equal amounts of soft white acrylic and a light tan acrylic. Add a tiny dot of white acrylic to each eye to give him a rather mischievous look.

Helmet — Dark brown acrylic and metallic gold
Horns — Light ivory acrylic
Face — Deep portrait pink acrylic
Hair — Soft white and light tan acrylic mix
Eyes — Blue acrylic iris with black pupils

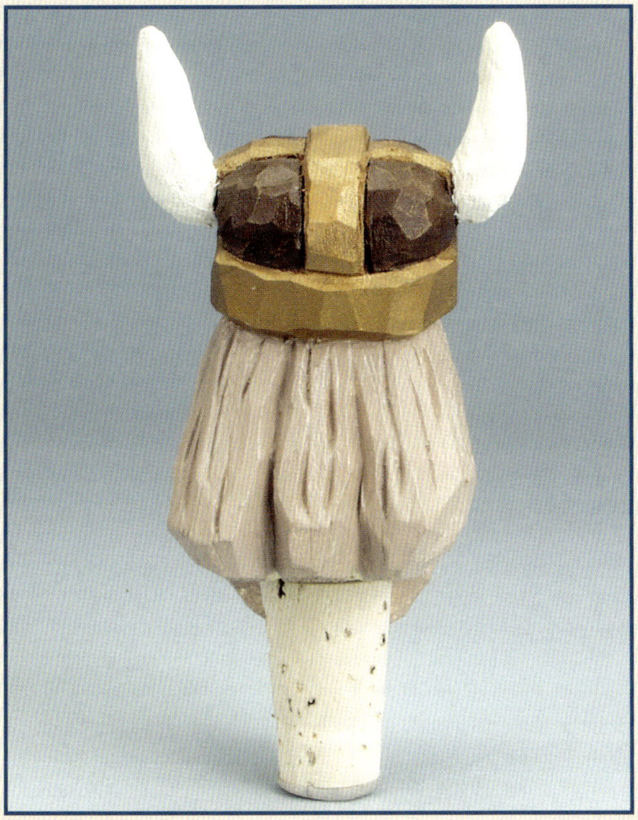

PATTERN

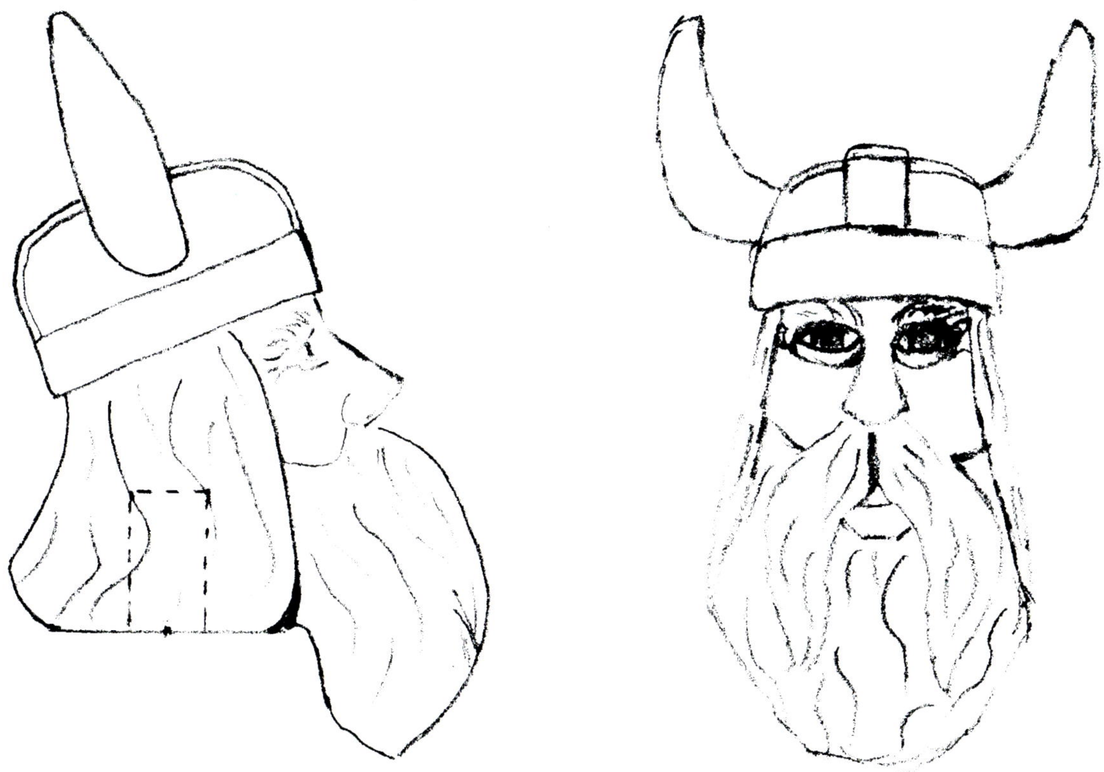

INTERMEDIATE

Mountain Man

TOOLS

Bench knife
1/4" v-tool
1/8" v-tool
5 mm #11 gouge
10 mm #7 gouge
3 mm #11 gouge
Woodburning pen (optional)

MATERIALS

Wood to fit pattern
3/8" hardwood dowel
Pre-drilled cork stopper

Carving Tips: First, take a pencil and draw a center line down the center of the face, top of his hat, and down the back of his hat. With a bench knife, round the corners of the cutout, leaving the nose area on the front of the figure alone for now. Looking at a side view, use the pencil to draw the edge of the fur-hooded hat that frames the face and beard. Be sure to do both side views. Looking at a front view, notice how the fur hat arches over the face, and draw this line as well. Continuing with the pencil, sketch the ear lines on top of his hat.

With the bench knife, create a stop cut along the hat lines that you have just drawn. Carve up to the stop cuts for the hat along the sides of the mountain man's face and above his forehead. Still using the bench knife, narrow the face and cut the large facial planes from the sides of the nose sloping downhill toward the sides of his face at the hat line. With the bench knife, create stop cuts along the ear lines and then carve away the waste wood from around the ears. Use the bench knife to round and shape the hat and backs of his ears. To hollow out the fronts of the ears, lay the bench knife flat on its side on top of the head and then create a stop cut within the inside base of each ear. Starting at the inside top of the ear, use the 5 mm #11 to carve down to the stop cut, hollowing out the ears. Refer to page 64 for instructions on carving faces.

Referring to the pattern, draw the nose and eye slits on his fur hat. Use a 1/8" v-tool to carve these features. To texture his fur hat use the 1/8" v-tool or a woodburning pen.

Painting Tips: Paint the beard and eyebrows with a storm gray acrylic as a base color; then paint lightly over the base coat with a soft white acrylic. A tiny white acrylic dot is added to each eye to bring the mountain man to life.

Hat — Burnt umber acrylic
Face — Deep portrait pink acrylic
Beard and Eyebrows — Storm gray with soft white acrylic
Eyes — Blueberry acrylic iris with black pupil

PATTERN

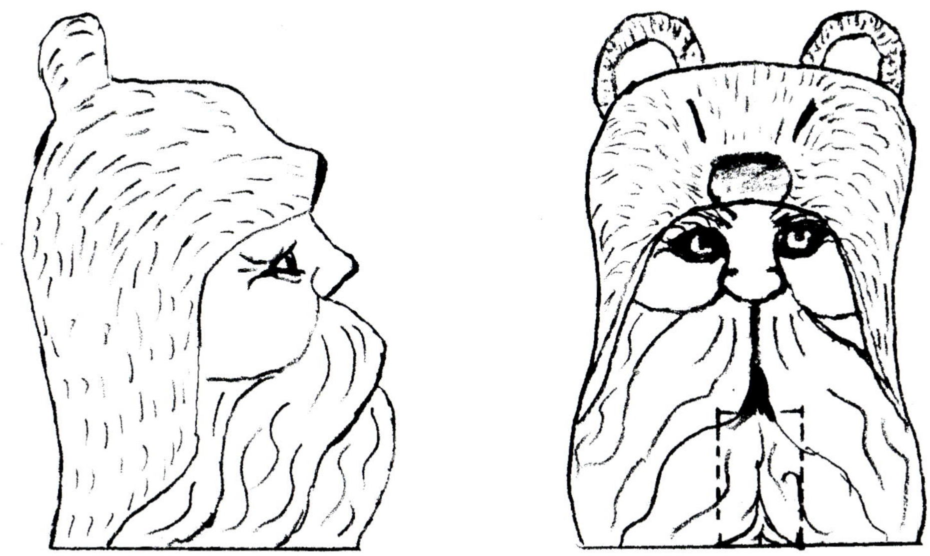

ADVANCED

Santa Stopper

TOOLS

Bench knife
1/8" v-tool
1/4" v-tool
Detail knife
5/8" #2 palm gouge
5 mm #7 gouge
5/8" #3 palm gouge
4 mm u-gouge
Woodburning tool (optional)

MATERIALS

Wood to fit pattern
3/8" hardwood dowel
Pre-drilled cork stopper

Carving Tips: Draw a centerline up the front, over the top and down the back of the cutout. Pencil in the upper and lower brim lines and the bottom of the ball on the top of the hat.

Knock off the corners of the cutout with the bench knife; then redraw any pencil lines that you may have carved away. Use the 1/4" v-tool to establish stop cuts along the upper and lower hat brim lines. With the tip of the bench knife, deepen these stop cuts.

Leaving the hat, brim and the ball on the top of the hat alone for the moment, use the bench knife or 5/8" #2 palm gouge to remove wood around Santa's head. Taper these cuts just enough to create the illusion of the head tucking up into the hat. Start about one inch below the hat and carve up to the brim.

Using the same tools, round and shape the head, removing any saw-marked surfaces as you go. Also carve the large angular facial planes on both sides of the nose. Be sure to leave the centerline that runs down the nose in place.

Draw the hairline on both sides of the figure. With the 1/4" v-tool, carve stop cuts along the pencil lines. Use the bench knife to remove a small amount of wood up to the hairline on both sides of the face.

Create stop cuts with the bench knife on both sides of the nose. Be sure to make the stop cut deepest at the point where the side of the nose intersects with the inner brow ridge line. Using the 5/8" #3 palm gouge, carefully push the tool in along one of the brow ridge lines to create a stop cut. Make sure the brow line stop cut is deepest at the point where the brow ridge intersects with the side of the nose. Carve away the waste wood with the bench knife.

Slide the tip of the detail knife under the bottom corner of the nose and create a stop cut. Carve down to the stop cut with the bench knife. Continue to use the bench knife to round the sharp edges on both sides of Santa's nose. Use the detail knife to round the nose up to the brow ridge. Separate the brows with a 4 mm u-gouge.

From the bottom corner of one side of the nose, draw a drooping arc over to the hairline on the side of the face. Carefully draw a matching

(continued on page 66.)

PATTERN

MASTER

arc on the opposite side. These arcs mark the cheek masses. Using the tip of the bench knife, create fairly deep stop cuts along these lines. Switch to a 5/8" #3 palm gouge. Starting just below the stop cuts, carve up to the stop cuts to remove wood and define the cheek masses. Round off the bottom edges of the cheek masses with the bench knife.

Use a pencil to draw moustache lines and the bottom mouth line. These lines create a small mouth triangle. Following the inside moustache lines and the line that marks the bottom of the mouth, create deep stop cuts with a bench knife. Angle these cuts toward the center of the mouth triangle. Re-cut these stop cuts until the little chip inside the mouth triangle pops out. Carve the moustache lines with a 1/4" v-tool. Deepen these lines with the bench knife. Finally, remove some wood from just outside the outer moustache lines and from just inside the inner moustache lines.

Draw the eye according to the pattern. With the tip of a very sharp detail knife, create a stop cut along the upper and lower eyeball lines. Cut straight in and make sure that the stop cuts are a little deeper in both the outside and inside corners of the eyeball. Laying the detail knife nearly flat across the surface of the eyeball, slide the tip of the knife into the corner of the eyeball, removing a small chip of wood. Do this for the inside and outside corners of both eyes. Again holding the knife nearly flat across the surface of the eyeball, round and shape the eyeball by removing small slivers of wood.

With a 1/8" v-tool, carve a stop cut along the pencil line for the lower eyelid. Define the upper eyelid with the v-tool. Use the 10mm #7 gouge to remove a small amount of wood from just below the lower eyelid.

Carve nostril lines on the sides of the nose with the 1/8" v-tool. Use a detail knife to create the stop cuts for the nostrils at the bottom of the nose. Scoop out the waste wood inside the nostrils with the 4 mm u-gouge.

Round the hat brim, the hat and the ball on the top of the hat with the bench knife. Pencil in the spiral lines on the hat; then carve them with the 1/4" v-tool. Texture the hat brim and the ball on the top of the hat with the 4 mm u-gouge.

Carve the beard and the hair with the 1/8" v-tool. Add additional texture with the 1/8" v-tool or a woodburner.

Painting Tips: When the black cherry acrylic paint on the hat has dried, dry brush metallic gold acrylic paint over its surface. Add a black pupil to each eye; then use a toothpick to add a tiny white highlight to each pupil.

Hat — Black cherry
Hat Brim and Ball — Metallic gold
Face — Deep portrait pink
Top Coat for Beard, Hair and Eyebrows — Light ivory
Base Coat for Beard, Hair and Eyebrows — Storm gray
Eyes — White
Iris — Blueberry

PATTERN

NOTE: Alterations can be made to the basic Santa pattern. Carve this Wind Swept Santa following the same general instructions for the Santa Stopper.

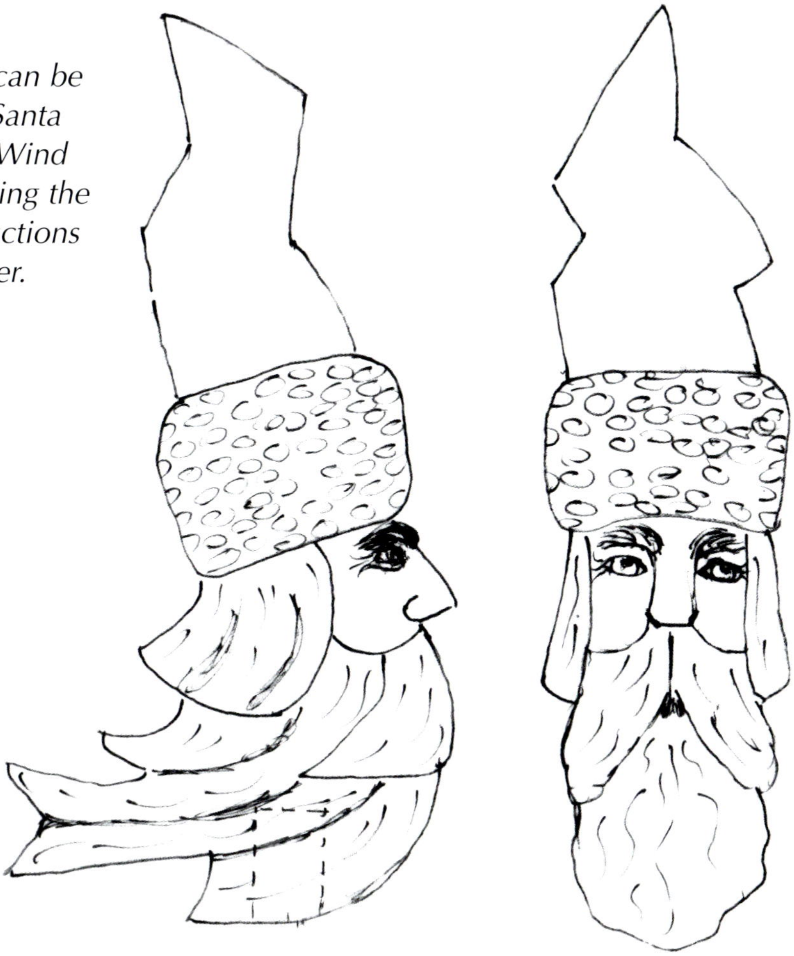